SHAKESPEARE'S
GRAMMAR

SHAKESPEARE'S GRAMMAR

Jonathan Hope

The Arden website is at
http://www.ardenshakespeare.com

Published in 2003 by The Arden Shakespeare
Copyright © 2003 Jonathan Hope

Shakespeare's Grammar

The Arden Shakespeare is an imprint of Thomson Learning

Thomson Learning
High Holborn House
50–51 Bedford Row
London WC1R 4LR

Typeset by Wyvern 21 Ltd, Bristol
Printed in Great Britain by T J International Ltd, Padstow

British Library Cataloguing in Publication Data
A catalogue record for this book is available from the British Library
Library of Congress Cataloging in Publication Data
A catalogue record has been requested

ISBN 1-903-43636-2

THE AUTHOR

JONATHAN HOPE is Reader in Literary Linguistics at Strathclyde University in Glasgow. His publications include *The Authorship of Shakespeare's Plays* (Cambridge University Press, 1994) and *Stylistics* (with Laura Wright, Routledge, 1996). He is Linguistics Adviser to the Arden Shakespeare, and is currently working on a book for the Arden Critical Companions Series to be entitled *Shakespeare and Language*.

To my grandparents

Robert Watson Hope

(born 2 October 1914)

Lilian Richardson

(born 21 April 1915)

James Rayner Lamb

(born 31 December 1915)

Dorothy Bowman

(born 17 November 1916)

CONTENTS

SYMBOLS AND ABBREVIATIONS

SYMBOLS

Symbol		Example
[ ]	encloses phonetic symbol	[θ]
*	marks ungrammatical form	*he doth goes
?	marks dubious form	?thou goes
^	indicates deletion, omission, or zero form	what ^ man thou art

ABBREVIATIONS

F	First Folio
F2	Second Folio
Q	First Quarto
Q2	Second Quarto
Q3	Third Quarto
OED	*Oxford English Dictionary* (2nd edition, 1989)

ABBREVIATIONS OF WORKS BY SHAKESPEARE

AC	*Antony and Cleopatra*
AW	*All's Well That Ends Well*
AYL	*As You Like It*
CE	*The Comedy of Errors*
Cor	*Coriolanus*
Cym	*Cymbeline*
Ham	*Hamlet*
1H4	*King Henry IV, Part 1*
2H4	*King Henry IV, Part 2*
H5	*King Henry V*
1H6	*King Henry VI, Part 1*
2H6	*King Henry VI, Part 2*
3H6	*King Henry VI, Part 3*
H8	*King Henry VIII*
JC	*Julius Caesar*
KJ	*King John*
KL	*King Lear*
LC	*A Lover's Complaint*
LLL	*Love's Labour's Lost*
Luc	*The Rape of Lucrece*

MA	*Much Ado about Nothing*
Mac	*Macbeth*
MM	*Measure for Measure*
MND	*A Midsummer Night's Dream*
MV	*The Merchant of Venice*
MW	*The Merry Wives of Windsor*
Oth	*Othello*
Per	*Pericles*
PT	*The Phoenix and the Turtle*
R2	*King Richard II*
R3	*King Richard III*
RJ	*Romeo and Juliet*
Son	*Sonnets*
TC	*Troilus and Cressida*
Tem	*The Tempest*
TGV	*The Two Gentlemen of Verona*
Tim	*Timon of Athens*
Tit	*Titus Andronicus*
TN	*Twelfth Night*
TNK	*The Two Noble Kinsmen*
TS	*The Taming of the Shrew*
VA	*Venus and Adonis*
WT	*The Winter's Tale*

ACKNOWLEDGEMENTS

A work like this rests heavily on the scholarship of others, and I acknowledge my debts to E.A. Abbott and Matti Rissanen in the Introduction. Inevitably, there are more general debts – for help with individual points, and for simple encouragement at times when it seemed I had taken on an impossible task. So very sincere and grateful thanks to: David Scott Kastan and Jessica Hodge, who should both take much of the blame; various Arden 3 editors, whose questions have probably helped me more than my answers have helped them; Gordon McMullan, for not talking about an interesting section of *A Winter's Tale*; Simon Palfrey, for asking me for an analysis of *Macbeth* 1.7.1–2; Jennifer Smith, queen of the Northern Personal Pronoun Rule, who saved me from making a fool of myself in section 2.1.8a; Nigel Fabb, who gave me a copy of H.C Wyld's *A History of Modern Colloquial English* (1921) just when I thought I was finished, which forced me into rewriting section 1.3.2j; Suzanne Trill and Lawrence Normand, who commented on sections of the *Grammar* and were very nice about it with hardly any prompting; four anonymous readers for Arden who gave me much to think about; Middlesex University and the Arts and Humanities Research Board, who supported this work by funding a sabbatical year for me. The final stages of work were made considerably easier by Hannah Hyam, who was an exceptionally careful and responsive copy editor.

JONATHAN HOPE
Strathclyde University,
Glasgow

INTRODUCTION

0.1 ABBOTT'S *GRAMMAR* AND *SHAKESPEARE'S GRAMMAR*

Shakespeare's Grammar was commissioned by the Arden Shakespeare as a replacement for E.A. Abbott's *A Shakespearian Grammar* (third edition, 1870). Few nineteenth-century books on Shakespeare have led such a long and active life: sales of 17,000 copies were claimed by 1883 (and at six shillings a copy, it was relatively expensive amongst educational books at the time); the book was constantly reprinted in the nineteenth and early twentieth centuries, was given a photographic facsimile reprint in 1966, appeared in electronic form on the *Arden Shakespeare CD-ROM* in 1997, and can now be found complete on the World Wide Web at http://www.perseus. tufts.edu/. Indeed, the afterlife of his *Grammar* is only eclipsed by that of another book by Abbott: the extraordinary social and mathematical science fiction fantasy, *Flatland: A Romance of Many Dimensions* (1884). The British Library has a 1960s edition of this, printed on a single strip of aluminium, and the book has been recommended by its modern editors as a good introduction to the imaginative difficulties of relativity and string theory, as well as the higher dimensional slicing phenomena encountered in the world of four-dimensional computer graphics.

Twentieth-century editors of Shakespeare knew Abbott's *Grammar* as the standard reference work on the syntax of Shakespeare's English, but it was first published by Macmillan in their School Class Books series: a textbook aimed at nineteenth-century schoolboys. Abbott, the son and father of headteachers, was a precociously young headmaster of the City of London School, and a leading educational reformer. His *Grammar* was intended to supply teaching materials for vernacular language classes, replacing (or at least complementing) classics lessons. It is thus an important text in the history of the creation of 'English' as a school subject, but perhaps an unusual one to have survived for over a hundred years as the highest authority on a central aspect of Shakespeare's achievement.

Although Abbott's *Grammar* is a dauntingly monumental piece of research, expanded by the apparently indefatigable Abbott from the 136 pages of the first edition in 1869 to 511 pages in the second edition of just a year later, it has serious shortcomings as a reference grammar of Shakespeare. First and foremost, it lacks any kind of linguistic structural organization. Instead, the book consists of a series of sequentially numbered paragraphs, dealing with linguistic features in alphabetical order (so the book begins with twenty-two paragraphs on adjectives, and then moves on to adverbs). This has made reference to individual paragraphs simple, but prevents the book giving a coherent description of Early Modern English. Linguistic features are treated in isolation from each other, and the language of Shakespeare is seen as an atomized collection of divergences from Victorian English. The after-effects of this approach can be seen in the fragmented treatment of linguistic issues in editions of Shakespeare: grammatical glosses are rarely contextualized, and all too often a simple paragraph number from Abbott is used in lieu of a genuine explanation.

Inevitably given the date of composition, Abbott's work is characterized by some prescriptive attitudes to grammatical variation, and perhaps more surprisingly, he can be very casual in quoting Shakespeare; for example (see section 0.3 for referencing conventions):

> 'tis very possible hee'l scorne it, for the man (as you
> know all) hath a contemptible spirit   (Fp *MA* 2.3.175–6)

appears as

> 'Tis very probable that the man will scorn it, for he hath
> a very contemptible spirit.   (Abbott, paragraph 3)

This instance is unusually free in its alterations, but similar transformations occur throughout Abbott's *Grammar*. The alterations never affect the linguistic feature under discussion, so I presume they are the result of unconscious tidying in the process of recording and recopying examples. This said, the great strength of Abbott's work lies in the wealth of illustrative examples it provides for each linguistic feature. In preparing this new grammar, I often began with Abbott's text in electronic format, copying and pasting his examples into my structure, and providing my own account of the linguistic feature under discussion. I then replaced Abbott's quotations with quotations from the Folio or Quarto text.

My aim in writing this new grammar has been to produce an up-to-date, systematic descriptive grammar of Shakespeare which can be used by editors, teachers and students of Shakespeare, without assuming any detailed linguistic knowledge or familiarity with work in historical linguistics. I particularly wanted to present Shakespeare's idiolect (that is, his particular version of Early Modern English) within a coherent linguistic structure, so that readers could get a sense of the interrelatedness of many of the features of Early Modern English (see section 0.4). To some extent, this desire for coherence is at odds with my other aim: that of producing a reference grammar which editors, for example, can dip into to check if an unusual construction they encounter is likely to be a minority variant form or a textual error. I am also acutely conscious of the fact that linguistic scholars, and students of English in non-Anglophone systems, are likely to find much of this grammar overly basic, while literary scholars and students in Anglophone traditions, whose training does not necessarily include any formal language element, may find the pace unforgiving. Such tensions and worries are, I think, inevitable in a project of this kind, but I have tried to deal with them as best I can through the structure of the work, something I explain in the next section.

The conventionally recognized periods of English are as follows: **Old English** (*c.* 500–*c.* 1100); **Middle English** (*c.* 1100–*c.* 1450); **Early Modern English** (*c.* 1450–*c.* 1700). The final period, Modern English (*c.* 1700 to the present), is the least well defined (some scholars date it from 1800), and includes versions of English which we are likely to feel differ significantly from our own. I have therefore not used the term in this grammar, and refer throughout to **Present-day English**, by which I mean late twentieth and early twenty-first-century English.

0.2   USING *SHAKESPEARE'S GRAMMAR*: HOW TO FIND THINGS

A recurrent frustration of writing this grammar has been the fact that while reading, writing and understanding are largely linear activities, grammars are three-dimensional networks of interdependent connections and recursive loops. It seems logical to begin with **noun phrases**, and then move on to **verbs** and **clause** structure, until you remember that **relative clauses** need to be considered within noun-phrase structure, and clause **objects** tend to be noun phrases. The obvious place to consider **adjectives** seems at first to be within noun-phrase structure – but adjectives are also frequently found as independent elements in clause structure. I have spent far more time than I would have liked trying out different structures for this grammar, and for my pains have come to the conclusion that there is no good structure for a grammar of Shakespeare which assumes no knowledge on the part of its user, and therefore tries to educate as it explicates. I have also tried to address the problem of users who lack the technical vocabulary to describe the problem they have encountered, and who therefore cannot use an index, or know intuitively where the issue is likely to be discussed (the technical terms in bold print in this and the previous paragraph, and throughout the grammar, will be found defined in the glossary).

I have settled on a structure which divides utterances, apparently neatly, into noun phrases and **verb phrases**, so that the following utterance:

> Jove knowes what man thou might'st have made　　(F *Cym* 4.2.207)

would be represented thus:

(Jove)	(knows what man thou mightst have made)
noun phrase	*verb phrase*

The structure of noun phrases is covered in Part 1 of this grammar; that of the verb phrase in Part 2. All well and good, until it is noticed that the verb phrase here contains a **noun clause** ('what man thou might'st have made') and two other noun phrases ('what man', 'thou'). I have tried to deal with cases like this (and they are legion) with frequent forward and backward references – for which the dipping reader will have to forgive me. Generally, I explain new concepts briefly when they first occur, more fully at what seems to me to be the most logical point in the grammar, and also in the glossary. Technical terms are in bold on first appearance, or when they have not been encountered recently, as a reminder that they are defined in the glossary. I hope that this system will allow the different types of users to get the most from this grammar.

Readers will find that the two parts of the grammar ('The Noun Phrase' and 'The Verb Phrase') each begin with an 'Overview' section, giving an account of the stylistic and literary effects associated with this element of structure, and a brief account of the technical matters involved. These overview sections aim, in the 'Stylistics' sections, to show the reader why it might be worth knowing about noun phrases and verb phrases when considering how Shakespeare's texts work. The 'Structure' sections aim to give enough technical information to allow the reader to navigate through the much more detailed grammatical sections which follow. Ideally, those unfamiliar with grammatical description should begin by reading both overviews.

Users who want to go straight to a detailed section on a particular linguistic feature should use the Contents pages and the index. As well as the glossary of terms, a list of citations of Shakespeare by text are included at the end of the grammar.

0.3 CITATION OF TEXTS: SOURCES AND CONVENTIONS

Throughout, I quote directly from the Folio or Quarto text of Shakespeare, retaining almost all Early Modern spelling and punctuation. Readers used to encountering Shakespeare in modernized texts, such as those of the Arden Shakespeare, may find this practice initially disconcerting. It is, however, necessary in a work whose focus is the actuality of Early Modern English, and there are already enough layers between Shakespeare the writer and the Folio and Quarto texts without our adding another. Somewhat reluctantly, I have regularized some Early Modern printing practices such as long -*s*, *u/v* use, ligatures, and *i* for *j*. Especially in quotations of prose, I have tried to retain layout as far as possible, since proximity to the end of a line may affect spelling and therefore morphology. Of course, any representation of a text will misrepresent and distort to some degree.

The source for my quotations is the facsimiles on the *Arden Shakespeare CD-ROM* (1997). Where I repeat a quotation in a modified form (for example to illustrate alternative possible constructions), I modernize it to avoid the artificiality of making up false old spellings, and use a different font.

After each quotation I give a source and line reference; for example:

for their owne Credit sake (Fp *1H4* 2.1.71)

the region cloude (Q *Son* 33.12)

In the first example, the capital F indicates that the quotation is from the First Folio text; the 'p' that the passage is set as prose in the Folio; *1H4* is the abbreviation for *The First Part of Henry IV*; and this is followed by act, scene and line reference to the Arden 2 text as it appears on the *Arden Shakespeare CD-ROM*. In the second example, the passage is quoted from the First Quarto (Q) of the *Sonnets*, and the absence of 'p' indicates that it is set as verse. A full list of the abbreviations used for work titles, and other abbreviations and symbols used in the text, can be found on pp. xi–xii.

Underlinings in quotations from Shakespeare mark the word or words relevant to the linguistic issue under discussion.

References to Abbott are to the third edition as included on the *Arden Shakespeare CD-ROM*.

0.4　SHAKESPEARE'S LINGUISTIC CONTEXT

In the England of Shakespeare's childhood (though perhaps not in that of his adulthood), English was something of an upstart: serious science, theology and education were carried out in Latin; English had not long, and still not completely, replaced French as the language of government and the law; business records were routinely kept in a sophisticated macaronic mixture of all three languages. A standard written form of English was on its way, and some wrote explicitly about what it might be like, but the reality was a degree of variation in spelling and morphology which startles the modern reader on first encounter, and yet seems to have passed Early Modern users almost completely by. We live in an age of near-total literacy, where dictionaries and house styles rigorously police writing conventions. To us, English *is* writing: invariant and checkable; and adherence to the rules of the standard written language is an instant index (we suppose) of someone's intelligence or education. In 1564 there were rules (contrary to what some suggest, there were arguably *more* rules than there are today) but they were not a set of arbitrary rules conjured from misapplied logic, and imported foreign grammar. They were the real rules of language: the hard- and soft-wired rules all children learn without apparent effort, while sucking language in from the air around them. They were the rules of natural grammar – in flux, as always, and sometimes in competition with each other, with old and new alternatives vying for **semantic** and functional space.

These were some of the varying rules Shakespeare the child reconstructed from the language around him: at least two distinct ways of forming negatives and questions; multiple ways of inflecting verbs; the second person pronouns nearing the end of a 300-year shift from a system marking both number and case, through one based on politeness and social relationship, to one apparently marking nothing; a bewildering (to this grammarian at least) range of options for representing possession; generally a series of older **synthetic** systems surviving to a greater or lesser extent beside **analytic** alternatives. Variation and choice seemingly everywhere, where we have virtually none. No dictionaries as we understand them, and no descriptive grammars – no false sense that writing *is* language, and speaking a casual, secondary, pale imitation. Shakespeare grew up in, wrote in, a society which was primarily oral and aural, not one which was literate. The most significant 'publication' of his plays was their oral delivery in the theatre: in his lifetime, far more people would have *heard* them than would, or could, have *read* them.

Shakespeare began learning his English in 1564. He learned it, as is almost always the case, from older people who had learned theirs thirty to forty years before, and he learned it away from the major urban centres with their rapid rates of innovation and change, in a relatively conservative, rural area. The language Shakespeare learned had an unbroken oral and aural link with the language the Indo-Europeans spoke in prehistoric Europe (like him, and like us, their word for 'one' centred on a **nasal** [n]; for him, and for them, one of the ways to indicate that a noun was plural was to add an **alveolar fricative** [s] – as it still is for us). 'English' first arrived in the British Isles, not as a distinct language, but as a cluster of related dialects of Germanic, spoken by groups of northern European settlers who moved across the North Sea as the Roman empire withdrew from its western outpost. To a large extent, current British dialectal differences can be traced back to the different dialects of Germanic spoken by the settlers in different areas of Britain – and this is also true of much of the variation this grammar charts in Shakespeare's Early Modern English. This multiple dialectal origin for 'English' gave a pool of variation in Old English, Middle English and Early Modern English; variation which was steadily standardized out of the written language during the course of the sixteenth and seventeenth centuries.

Shakespeare lived at a crucial time in the history of English. Graphs charting a series of long-term changes in the grammar of English all show the years around 1600 as the point at which newer systems finally established themselves over older ones. At the same time, print culture was both accelerating standardization and allowing conventions to be fixed. Shakespeare's age and place of birth meant that he had access to both old and new grammatical forms. Younger, or more urban sixteenth-century writers than Shakespeare generally show much less variation in their grammar: their English is effectively closer to ours than Shakespeare's is. Intriguingly, this raises the possibility that Shakespeare's biography supplied him with a richer linguistic palate than other writers of his day. Investigation of this possibility is rapidly becoming feasible, with the availability of electronic texts and computer parsers of English, and the next stage in research from this grammar would be a series of comparative projects placing Shakespeare's idiolect in the context of those of his fellow writers.

0.5 FURTHER READING

I have not included any references to other linguistic work in the body of this grammar. My primary audience is not a historical linguistic one, and I felt that too much cross-referencing to other texts would make an already forbidding text too dense. I have therefore sought to give as straightforward and clear account of each linguistic feature as possible, without referring to many of the theoretical and descriptive debates ongoing in the field of the history of English. This means that I present a falsely monolithic account. I hope that my primary users – editors and students of Shakespeare – will find this the most useful approach. I hope too, however, that a small proportion of those users will be interested in the linguistics of Early Modern English enough to want to read further, and perhaps undertake work in what is a fascinating, vibrant, but still under-researched area.

The first port of call for anyone wanting to read more about Early Modern English should be Charles Barber's *Early Modern English* (Edinburgh University Press, second edition, 1996). This book, originally published in 1976, remains a model of accessibility and authority. More technical and comprehensive accounts of Early Modern and Middle English will be found in the chapters by Matti Rissanen and Olga Fischer in volumes 3 and 2 respectively of *The Cambridge History of the English Language* (Cambridge University Press, 1999 and 1992, general editor Richard Hogg). Matti Rissanen's chapter has informed this grammar on almost every page, and it is rightly regarded as the standard account of Early Modern English. Those interested in a historical stylistic approach, which I sketch in sections 1.0a and 2.0a, should read Sylvia Adamson's chapters on 'Literary Language' in *The Cambridge History of the English Language*, volumes 3 and 4 (1999). Sylvia Adamson is also one of the editors of a sister volume to this grammar, *Reading Shakespeare's Dramatic Language: A Guide* (Arden Shakespeare, 2001), which is aimed at literary students of Shakespeare, and covers language and rhetoric.

Issues surrounding the standardization of English are addressed by the essays in Laura Wright (ed.), *The Development of Standard English, 1300–1800* (Cambridge University Press, 2000). Brian Vickers's monumental *Shakespeare, Co-Author* (Oxford University Press, 2002) recovers for the scholarly tradition a wealth of previous work on attribution, much of it language-related.

After many years of relative neglect, Shakespearean scholars are turning their attention to language: Frank Kermode, *Shakespeare's*

Language (Penguin, 2000); Russ McDonald, *Shakespeare and the Arts of Language* (Oxford University Press, 2001); Lynne Magnusson, *Shakespeare and Social Dialogue* (Cambridge University Press, 1999). And there have even been two books on the fascinating subject of sound: Bruce R. Smith, *The Acoustic World of Early Modern England* (Chicago University Press, 1999) and Wes Folkerth, *The Sound of Shakespeare* (Routledge, 2002).

Finally, I should mention Norman Blake's *A Grammar of Shakespeare's Language* (Palgrave, 2002). The English-speaking world having waited 130 years for a grammar of Shakespeare to replace Abbott, it is perhaps typical that two should come along almost at once. I had planned and completed much of this grammar when Blake's came out, and I decided, for better or worse, not to look at it too closely until I had finished my own. In the event, we have taken very different approaches, with different audiences in mind, and Blake covers much material beyond the clause that I have, perhaps overly austerely, excluded (see, for example, his chapters on 'Discourse and Register' and 'Pragmatics'). I hope students and editors will find that the two grammars complement each other.

PART 1

THE NOUN PHRASE

OVERVIEW: THE STYLISTICS OF NOUN PHRASE USE

The final scene of Act 1 of *Macbeth* opens with the first of Macbeth's great soliloquies:

> If it were done, when tis done, then twer well,
> It were done quickly: If th'Assassination
> Could trammell up the Consequence, and catch
> With his surcease, Successe: that but this blow
> Might be the be all, and the end all. Heere,
> But heere, upon this Banke and Schoole of time,
> Wee'ld jumpe the life to come   (F *Mac* 1.7.1–7)

Macbeth has heard the witches prophesy that he will be king; Duncan has just made his fatal entrance into Macbeth's castle; and Macbeth now begins to manifest his equally fatal fascination with guilt and the consequences of deeds. The language here, as often in *Macbeth*, has a tantalizing, elusive quality. It appears to be concrete, plain, clear – concerned with the things of the world, and laying them out for consideration – but it constantly shears off into the puzzling and the ungraspable, into insubstantiality and darkness. The effects of this passage can be traced to the uses it makes of **noun phrases**, and, like much else in this play, these uses shift swiftly. (As with all technical terms in bold print, for a definition of **noun phrase** see the glossary or the relevant section of the grammar: in this case, 1.0b.)

The noun phrases in the first line and a half could hardly be more simple (I have underlined them in the following quotation):

> If <u>it</u> were done, when <u>tis</u> done, then <u>twer</u> well,
> <u>It</u> were done quickly   (F *Mac* 1.7.1–2)

Four noun phrases, each one consisting of the simple **pronoun** *it* (see section 1.3.2 for more on pronouns); note, however, that in two cases the vowel is elided and the pronoun is joined to the following word ('tis' = *it is*; 'twer' = *it were*). But this apparent structural simplicity does not entail **semantic** simplicity. The language is condensed here: we are not used to this frequency of **pronoun replacement**, especially in the context of the opening of a scene. Normally, pronouns refer back to an **antecedent**, something which has been mentioned previously, and which a reader, or listener, can easily recover. Here though, readers and listeners have to work harder than usual: the antecedent of the first, second, and fourth *it* forms can be found, not in this scene, but at the end of 1.5, where Lady Macbeth greets her husband, and his news of the arrival of Duncan. She knows that in order for Macbeth to come to the throne they must kill the King:

> He that's comming,
> Must be provided for: and you shall put
> This Nights great Businesse into my dispatch   (F *Mac* 1.5.66–8)

'This Nights great Businesse' is the murder of Duncan (and it is perhaps prophetic of Lady Macbeth's ultimate destruction by guilt that she uses a euphemism even here), and it is also a noun phrase, equivalent to 'the murder', and the antecedent of Macbeth's 'it'.

The lack of an explicit **referent** for the *it* forms at the start of 1.7 gives the impression that we are overhearing someone in the middle of thought. We are plunged into an ongoing personal debate, and we assume that the referent has been made explicit at some earlier point. However, Macbeth's failure to name his intended deed directly could also be taken as an indication that he already has doubts about it. His language makes a show of approaching his topic, but then always veers away into some kind of insubstantiality: either uncertain reference as here, or abstractness, which is what happens when he shifts from pronouns to full noun phrases halfway through line 2:

> If th'Assassination
> Could trammell up the Consequence, and catch
> With his surcease, Successe   (F *Mac* 1.7.2–4)

In these lines, we have four noun phrases, each with a **noun** as **head** (see section 2.1.0): 'th'Assassination', 'the Consequence', 'his surcease' and 'Successe'. So, on one level, we have more explicit reference: there is no pronoun replacement. But even here, the language, through the chosen nouns, seems to work to keep the reality of what Macbeth is contemplating at bay. All of the nouns are ultimately derived from Latin or French words, marking them out as **high-register items** in English, and tending to increase their separation from everyday life. Indeed, 'Assassination' would have struck the ears of *Macbeth*'s first audiences as a particularly unusual noun: the *OED* cites this as its first appearance in English; and 'surcease' and 'Successe' were relatively new to the language too (though it is important to remember that *OED* first citations are merely indicative of a word's first use: they should not be taken as proof of first use, since spoken uses are lost to us; manuscript ones were not searched by the *OED* readers; printed texts do not all survive, and those that do were not exhaustively searched).

The literary effects created in these four lines, then, can be linked to the grammatical, structural and semantic properties of the noun phrases used – and I have been arguing that similar literary effects (a sense of dislocation and uncertain reference, and a failure to engage substantially with the issues raised) are produced by different linguistic features (initially pronoun replacement, and then the use of high-register, innovative nouns). Shakespeare is manipulating the stylistic potential of English noun phrase structure in a highly subtle and sophisticated way here – and if we want to analyse and discuss it systematically, we need a set of descriptive grammatical terms such as are laid out in this grammar.

Moving back to Macbeth's speech, the next four lines show a further change in the type of noun phrase employed:

> that but <u>this blow</u>
> Might be <u>the be all</u>, and <u>the end all</u>. Heere,
> But heere, upon <u>this Banke and Schoole of time</u>,
> Wee'ld jumpe <u>the life to come</u>   (F *Mac* 1.7.4–7)

Where lines 2–4 (from 'If th'Assassination' to 'Successe') used nouns derived exclusively from Latin and French sources, all of the nouns here are part of the core, Old English derived vocabulary (note that all of the nouns in lines 2–4 are polysyllabic, while all of these are monosyllables). Shakespeare seems to be very fond of such contrasts in register – and perhaps especially so in *Macbeth*. Normally, linguists would predict that a shift from Latin and French to Old English derived nouns would result in more concrete imagery, but here I do not think that such a shift in effect occurs: 'this blow' seems basic enough, but the use of the **demonstrative** 'this' serves to dislocate the audience, since we have not encountered 'this blow' before. The next two noun phrases, 'the be all' and 'the end all', consist of simple enough words, but their structure is highly unusual: their heads seem to be made up of **verb + determiner** compounds (*be* + *all* and *end* + *all*). They are very familiar to us, but would have jolted *Macbeth*'s early audiences: we know them because they have passed into the language from this first usage; would we have been able to understand them if we had first come across them spoken in the open air of the Globe?

The unfamiliarity of 'be all' and 'end all' seems to be abandoned in the next line with 'this Banke and Schoole of time', the longest noun phrase so far, and the first to have any kind of **modification** (the **prepositional phrase** 'of time'). There is a textual crux here, but either reading is consistent with my argument. The Folio text has 'Banke and Schoole', giving us a noun phrase with two coordinated concrete nouns as its head. Defenders of this reading see 'Banke' as law bench and 'Schoole' as law school, with this imagery leading into the following 'But in these <u>Cases</u>, / We still have <u>judgement</u> heere' (7–8). In the eighteenth century Theobald, however, suggested emending 'Schoole' to 'shoal' – and almost every modern edition follows this change, shifting the imagery from that of the law to the even more concrete arena of river geography. Whichever reading is accepted, the heads of this noun phrase are Old English in derivation and concrete in reference – so once again the language seems to gesture towards a stylistic change. But note the use of the abstract noun 'time' in the post-modifying prepositional phrase: the effect of this is once again to undermine the apparent concreteness of Macbeth's language, converting his concrete imagery into abstract through metaphor.

So we can describe the structural and semantic features of noun phrases using descriptive grammar, and use this description to analyse and discuss literary effect. In this passage, noun phrase structure builds steadily in complexity, the most complex noun phrases coming towards the end: 'Banke and Schoole of time' and 'the life to come'. It would be wrong, however, to assume that structurally simple noun phrases always produce simple language, or have limited stylistic potential. Linguists normally associate a high frequency of pronouns with relatively informal contexts: conversation, for example; but as we can see from Macbeth's speech, a high frequency of pronoun replacement can make it difficult for the recipient of a piece of language to make sense of it. Pronoun replacement depends on the recipient being able to recover the referent of the pronouns – it tends to rely on the participants in an exchange sharing a great deal of contextual information. So structural simplicity (in terms of noun phrases) is only gained at the expense of semantic or contextual complexity.

The passage also demonstrates the stylistic range available within the English lexicon: a core of Old English derived terms, generally with neutral or low stylistic weight, surrounded by layers of later borrowings from various languages, Latin and French most importantly, carrying more technical or formal, or abstract, connotations.

One major aspect of noun phrases almost entirely missing from Macbeth's soliloquy is **modification**. To some extent, this can be explained by the speech situation: Macbeth is, at least in theory, addressing himself, and however evasive he may be, we can assume that he knows what he means by such unmodified noun phrases as 'it' and 'this blow'. Speech situations where the participants do not share contextual information, or where new information is being communicated, are typified by more heavily modified noun phrases, as is shown by the 'recognition' scene in *The Winter's Tale*. Rather than staging the discovery of Perdita's true identity, which might have detracted from the force of the final reawakening of Hermione, Shakespeare has the recognition of Perdita reported by minor characters:

> *Gent.* 1.
> . . . Here comes a Gentleman, that happily knowes more:
> The Newes, *Rogero*.
> *Gent.* 2.   Nothing but Bon-fires: the Oracle is fulfill'd
> the Kings Daughter is found: such a deale of wonder is
> broken out within this houre, that Ballad-makers cannot   5
> be able to expresse it.   *Enter another Gentleman.*
> Here comes the Lady *Paulina's* Steward, hee can deliver
> you more. How goes it now (Sir.) This Newes (which
> is call'd true) is so like an old Tale, that the veritie of it is
> in strong suspition: Ha's the King found his Heire?   10
> *Gent.* 3.   Most true, if ever Truth were pregnant by
> Circumstance: That which you heare, you'le sweare
> you see, there is such unitie in the proofes. The Mantle
> of Queene *Hermiones*: her Jewell about the Neck of it:
> the Letters of *Antigonus* found with it, which they know   15
> to be his Character: the Maiestie of the Creature, in re-
> semblance of the Mother: the Affection of Noblenesse,
> which Nature shewes aboue her Breeding, and many o-
> ther Evidences, proclayme her, with all certaintie, to be
> the Kings Daughter   (Fp *WT* 5.2.20–40)

Here are the noun phrases from the passage, with modification underlined. The first list contains the noun phrases spoken by Gentlemen 1 and 2; the second contains those spoken by Gentleman 3:

Gentlemen 1 and 2
    a Gentleman, <u>that happily knowes more</u>
    The Newes
    Rogero
    Nothing
    Bon-fires
    the Oracle

the <u>Kings</u> Daughter
such a <u>deale of wonder</u>
this houre
Ballad-makers
it
the <u>Lady *Paulina's*</u> Steward
hee
you
more
it
Sir
This Newes <u>which is call'd true</u>
an <u>old</u> Tale
the veritie <u>of it</u>
strong suspition
the King
his Heire

Gentleman 3
Truth
Circumstance
That <u>which you heare</u>
such unitie <u>in the proofes</u>
The Mantle <u>of Queene *Hermiones*</u>
her Jewell <u>about the Neck of it</u>
the Letters <u>of *Antigonus* found with it, which they know to be his Character</u>
the Maiestie <u>of the Creature, in resemblance of the Mother</u>
the Affection <u>of Noblenesse, which Nature shewes above her Breeding</u>
many <u>other</u> Evidences
her
all certaintie
the <u>Kings</u> Daughter

There is an interesting contrast in the positioning and size of modification between the first half of the passage, where Gentlemen 1 and 2 speak, and the second half, where Gentleman 3 recounts the recognition. In the first half, what little modification there is tends to come before the noun, and consists of one or two words ('the <u>Kings</u> Daughter', 'an <u>old</u> Tale'). In the second half, most modification comes *after* the noun – and generally consists of much larger elements ('The Mantle <u>of Queene *Hermiones*</u>').

The reason for this is that there is a difference in the type of information communicated by the modification. In the first half of the passage, the information may be essential to understanding (we need to know that it is the *King's* daughter we are being told about), but it is largely generalized, conventional and expected. In the second half, the information is much more specific and unexpected. Shakespeare is not doing anything unusual here. The passage illustrates the way English naturally packages information: expected or **given information** tends to come early, in small structures; unexpected, **new information** comes late in much larger elements. This follows from the commonsense observation that we do not need to be given a lot of information about things we already know about.

In this overview section I have tried to give some indication of the stylistic range of the noun phrase in Early Modern English. Informal, or context-dependent, situations favour high frequencies of pronoun replacement and restricted modification. Information-heavy, less context-dependent exchanges favour more elaborate modification. Writers can further manipulate stylistic texture by moving between the Old English core of the English lexicon and the French and Latin derived loan words.

OVERVIEW: THE STRUCTURE OF THE NOUN PHRASE

Why have I been using the term 'the noun phrase' rather than just 'the noun'? This might appear an unnecessary complication, but in fact, it makes analysis of and comparisons between passages considerably easier. I have already claimed that the *it* forms used by Macbeth at the start of his soliloquy are **functionally equivalent** to Lady Macbeth's full noun phrase of two scenes earlier:

> If <u>it</u> were done, when <u>t</u>is done, then <u>t</u>wer well,
> <u>It</u> were done quickly
>
> (F *Mac* 1.7.1–2)

> He that's comming,
> Must be provided for: and you shall put
> <u>This Nights great Businesse</u> into my dispatch
>
> (F *Mac* 1.5.67–8)

The functional equivalence of these two one-word pronouns and single four-word phrase can be shown by the fact that they could all be substituted for each other in either context:

You shall put	(this night's great business)	into my hands
You shall put	(it)	into my hands
If	(it)	were done
If	(this night's great business)	were done

This functional equivalence suggests that while 'it' and 'this night's great business' might look very different, they are in fact examples of the same type of thing. Despite their disparities in size, they have exactly the same grammatical role: that of **object** in the first sentence, and **subject** in the second. Linguists use 'noun phrase' as the basic element of analysis when working with nouns in clause structure because any pronoun, or single unmodified noun, can be replaced by a functionally equivalent noun phrase – and vice versa.

A further advantage of using 'noun phrase' as a basic theoretical concept in analysis is illustrated by the increasing internal complexity of the noun phrases used above. 'It' is a pronoun, but 'this night's great business' consists of a **genitive**-phrase determiner ('this night's'), a pre-modifying **adjective** ('great'), and a head noun ('business'). Because noun phrases can vary so greatly in terms of their internal structure, while sharing a set of grammatical **functions**, it is very useful to have a single descriptive label to cover them all.

THE STRUCTURE OF THE NOUN PHRASE IN ENGLISH: PRE-HEAD, HEAD, POST-HEAD

In English, noun phrases must contain a **head** word, usually either a *pronoun* or a *noun*. Noun phrases also contain structural slots on either side of the head word into which various optional items can be placed (from single words to phrases, and even **clauses**). For the sake of simplicity, it is possible to consider noun phrase structure in terms of just three positions: *pre-head*, *head*, and *post-head*.

Pre-head	Head	Post-head	
	Viola		(F *TN* 5.1.251)
young	*Lorenzo*		(F *MV* 5.1.18)
The	*Thane*	of Cawdor	(F *Mac* 1.2.54)
a	Dagger,	which I see before me	(F *Mac* 2.1.33)
the inchanted	hearbs	That did renew old Eson	(F *MV* 5.1.13–14)

The optionality of the items in the slots on either side of the head is the reason noun phrases can vary so much in length and complexity. There are general tendencies for certain types of elements to appear in only one of these positions: **determiners** and **adjectives** tend to be pre-head, while **prepositional phrases** and various types of **clause** tend to be post-head.

Pre-head elements

The pre-head slot can contain *determiners* (such as *all, the, many, half*) and **pre-head modification** (most frequently made up of an **adjectival phrase**).

Determiners limit the reference of the head of the noun phrase in some way, most frequently to do with specificity (for example, *a* versus *the*) or number:

Determiner	Head	
halfe a	Fish	(Fp *Tem* 3.2.28)
both	thee and *Warwicke*	(F *3H6* 4.7.86)
th'one	halfe	(F *LLL* 2.1.130)
these	injunctions	(F *MV* 2.9.17)

Pre-modification can be made up of either adjectival phrases, nouns or verb forms:

adjective	to make us <u>publike</u> sport	(Fp *MW* 4.4.14)
noun	go and set <u>London</u> Bridge on fire	(Fp *2H6* 4.6.12–13)
verb -ing	with a <u>rising</u> sigh	(F *1H4* 3.1.8)
verb -en	Raze out the <u>written</u> troubles of the Braine	(F *Mac* 5.3.42)
	In grosse Rebellion, and <u>detested</u> Treeson	(F *R2* 2.3.108)

(Note that the term *-en* **forms** covers verb forms with an *-ed* ending as well as ones with an *-en* ending: see section 1.2.7.)

Determiners and pre-modification are covered in more detail in sections 1.1.0–1.2.9.

The head

As mentioned above, in English, noun phrases must contain a *head* word, almost always either a pronoun or a noun, but more rarely an adjective or determiner:

noun	Mine <u>Eyes</u> are full of <u>Teares</u>	(F *R2* 4.1.244)
pronoun	<u>I</u> knew <u>you</u> at the first	(F *TS* 2.1.196)
adjective	the bottome of the <u>deepe</u>	(F *1H4* 1.3.201)
determiner	I knew you at the <u>first</u>	(F *TS* 2.1.196)

Noun phrase heads are covered in more detail in sections 1.3.0–5.

Post-head elements

Post-head modifiers generally consist of prepositional phrases or **relative clauses** (**finite** and **non-finite**), and more rarely adjectival phrases and noun phrases:

prepositional phrase	A pound <u>of flesh</u>	(F *MV* 4.1.228)
relative clause (finite)	a man, <u>who hath a daughter</u>	(Fp *WT* 4.2.42–3)
relative clause (non-finite)	The danger <u>formerly by me rehearst</u>	(F *MV* 4.1.358)
adjectival phrase	things precious	(F *Cor* 2.2.125)
noun phrase	*Cinna* <u>the Poet</u>	(F *JC* 3.3.29)

Post-head elements are covered in more detail in sections 1.4.0–4.

1.1

PRE-HEAD ELEMENTS: DETERMINERS

1.1.0 OVERVIEW

Type: all   the   a   my   <u>Cresseds</u> Uncle   many

Determiners restrict, or determine, the reference of the head noun in some way. Most typically they do this by number (e.g. *one, all, every, no*), specificity (*a, the, this, that*), or possession (by possessive pronouns such as *thy* and *my*, and possessive noun phrases of the type '<u>Jonathan's</u> book').

This overview section gives an account of determiner behaviour common to Early Modern English and Present-day English (sections 1.1.0a–g); subsequent sections (1.1.1–3) analyse differences in the determiner system between the two states of the language.

1.1.0a Articles

Type: the (definite)   a, an (indefinite)

The distinction between **definite** and **indefinite articles** functions as in Present-day English:

Host.   You will not pay for <u>the</u> glasses you have burst?
Beg.   No, not <u>a</u> deniere   (Fp *TS* Induction 1.6–7)

1.1.0b Demonstratives

Type: this   that
        these   those
        yon   yond   yonder

Demonstratives are **deictic**, or pointing, terms. They distinguish number (*this/these*) and distance (*this/these* = close; *that/those* = distant). Distance may be spatial or temporal (for example 'these days' and 'those days').

1.1.0c Possessives

Type: my   thy   your   his   her   it   our   their

           Cresseds Uncle

Possessives consist of possessive pronouns (covered in sections 1.3.2a–j) and **genitive** noun phrases:

possessive pronouns
My Lord, your sonne, made me to think of this   (F AW 1.3.227)

genitive noun phrase
I am Cresseds Uncle, / That dare leave two together   (F AW 2.1.96–7)

Possessive constructions in Early Modern English show a complex range of possible realizations, and these are covered in detail in section 1.1.3.

1.1.0d Interrogatives

Type: what   which

Interrogatives such as *what* and *which* function as determiners when they introduce questions. *What* has two forms:

interrogative   What bloody man is that?   (F Mac 1.2.1)

exclamative   What a haste lookes through his eyes?   (F Mac 1.2.46)

1.1.0e Quantifiers

Type: some   any   no   many

Quantifiers specify the head of the noun phrase in terms of the amount present. Section 1.1.1 details the development of quantifiers from adjectives, and some consequent differences between the Early Modern and Present-day quantifier systems.

1.1.0f Numerals

Type: one   two   three . . .

Numerals specify number, and in many languages (for example French, Spanish) the words for *one* and the indefinite article are the same. This used to be the case in English, and this explains some Early Modern usages of *a/an* (see section 1.1.2a).

1.1.0g Ordinals

Type: first   second   third . . .

The ordinals function as they do in Present-day English:

the <u>first</u> choice   (Fp *WT* 4.4.314)

My <u>second</u> Joy   (F *WT* 3.2.96)

My <u>third</u> comfort   (F *WT* 3.2.98)

and as in Present-day English, *first* often appears as the head on a noun phrase (see section 1.3.0):

My last good deed, was to entreat his stay,
What was my <u>first</u>?   (F *WT* 1.2.97–8)

First can also function as an **adverbial** rather than a determiner:

let's <u>first</u> see moe Ballads   (Fp *WT* 4.4.274)

1.1.1 DEVELOPMENT OF DETERMINERS FROM ADJECTIVES

Type: I have wept a hundred <u>several</u> times

Although nominally a **closed class** of **function words**, determiners are closely related to adjectives, and their use in English shows a certain amount of change and development. The development of determiners from adjectives can be illustrated by the behaviour of *several*. In Present-day English, *several* is a full determiner (a quantifier), semantically equivalent to *a few* or *some*. In the Early Modern period, however, it is a full adjective with the meaning of 'divided', 'separate', 'different' – from its root in the verb *to sever*:

Ile kisse each <u>severall</u> paper, for amends   (F *TGV* 1.2.109)

That is, 'I will kiss each separate piece of paper'.

I have wept a hundred <u>severall</u> times   (F *TGV* 4.4.143)

That is, 'I have wept a hundred different times'.

I suffered the pangs of three <u>severall</u> deaths   (Fp *MW* 3.5.108–9)

That is, 'I have suffered the pains of three different deaths'.
Note that in Present-day English the determiner combinations

'each several' and 'three several' are impossible – as is 'a hundred several times'. The apparent Present-day English equivalent, 'several hundred times', means something quite different: 'several' is a determiner modifying 'hundred', rather than an adjective modifying 'times'. Shakespeare never uses *several* in its modern, full determiner sense; only as an adjective:

> Good morrow masters, each his <u>severall</u> way   (F *MA* 5.3.29)

That is, '(Let) each (go) his different way'.

> My lips are no Common, though <u>severall</u> they be   (F *LLL* 2.1.222)

Note that 'several' here is the **complement** of 'to be' – a fully adjectival function.

> they'll know
> By favours <u>severall</u>, which they did bestow   (F *LLL* 5.2.124–5)

Again, 'several' is fully adjectival, showing **postpositive** *head + adjective* order (see section 1.4.4).

When King Lear declares

> We have this hour a constant will to publish
> Our daughters <u>severall</u> Dowers   (F *KL* 1.1.42–3)

he is stating that each daughter has a *different* dower, not that they all have more than one, as a Present-day English reading would imply!

It is interesting to note that in Early Modern English, *diverse* sometimes functions in the quantifier role of Present-day *several*, filling what might otherwise be a semantic gap:

> we lay these Honours on this man,
> To ease our selves of divers sland'rous loads   (F *JC* 4.1.19–20)

where the sense is 'some' or 'a few', rather than 'different', as Present-day usage of *diverse* would have it. *Diverse* is similarly frequently used in stage directions for entries of unspecified numbers of minor characters:

> *Enter the King of France with Letters, and*
> *divers Attendants.*   (F *AW* 1.2.1)

The meaning is that the precise number of actors required is vague – not that they should represent a cross-section of ages, classes, or races!

For determiners used as the heads of noun phrases, see section 1.3.4.

1.1.2 DETERMINERS USED IN DIFFERENT COMBINATIONS OR IN DIFFERENT SENSES

Type: they are of <u>a</u> mind
        <u>each his</u> needless heavings

(Abbott, 12, 79–81)

It is possible to combine determiners, although there are constraints on the order in which they can be combined:

I would not from your love make <u>such a</u> stray   (F *KL* 1.1.209)

                For we
Haue <u>no such</u> Daughter   (F *KL* 1.1.261–2)

but not

   *I would not from your love make <u>a such</u> stray
   *For we have <u>such no</u> daughter

These constraints are not always the same in Early Modern English as they are today, hence (Abbott, 87):

<u>a many</u> merry men   (Fp *AYL* 1.1.115)

<u>A many thousand</u> warlike French   (F *KJ* 4.2.199)

But <u>many a many</u> foot of Land the worse   (F *KJ* 1.1.183)

1.1.2a *A/an* in the sense of *one/the same*

The indefinite articles *a* and *an* are originally derived from the numeral *one*. This sense is still available in Early Modern English, producing instances where the indefinite articles carry much more stress than is possible in Present-day English, with the article synonymous with *one* or *the same*:

            He and his Phisitions
   Are of <u>a</u> minde   (F *AW* 1.3.232–3)

That is, 'He and his physicians are of the same mind'. Similarly:

my selfe, and a sister, both born in <u>an</u> houre   (Fp *TN* 2.1.18–19)

'fore God they are both in <u>a</u> tale   (Fp *MA* 4.2.29–30)

That is, 'born within the same hour' and 'they are both telling the same story'.

Instances where *a* has a strong sense of *one*:

and two men ride of <u>a</u> horse, one must ride behind   (Qp *MA* 3.5.35–6)

That is, 'If two men ride one horse, one must ride behind'.

For in <u>a</u> night the best part of my powre
As I upon advantage did remove,
Were in the *Washes* all unwarily,
Devoured   (F *KJ* 5.7.61–4)

You, or any man living, may be drunk at <u>a</u> time, man
                                                    (Fp *Oth* 2.3.304–5)

These Foyles haue all <u>a</u> length   (F *Ham* 5.2.262)

1.1.2b *Each/every/one* for *each of/every one of/none of*

Present-day English does not allow quantifiers such as *each*, *every* and *none* to occur immediately next to demonstratives or possessive determiners; for example:

*each her irritating habits

Instead, Present-day English introduces a complex determiner structure with an *of* prepositional phrase:

each <u>of</u> her irritating habits

This is not required in Early Modern English:

At each his needlesse heavings   (F *WT* 2.3.35)

                    Of every
These happend accidents   (F *Tem* 5.1.249–50)

none our parts   (F *AC* 1.3.36)

1.1.2c *Each* and *everyone* + *noun* treated as plurals

Present-day English tends to regard quantifiers such as *each* and *everyone* as specifying the separate identities of the members of a group, and consequently they trigger singular agreement:

each goe<u>s</u> home

even though more than one individual is involved. Early Modern

English often treats these quantifiers as plural:

> And <u>each</u> (though enimes to ethers raigne)
> <u>Doe</u> in consent shake hands to torture me   (Q *Son* 28.5–6)

> <u>Each</u> in her sleepe themselves so <u>beautifie</u>   (Q *Luc* 404)

> every thing
> In readiness for *Hymenous* <u>stand</u>   (F *Tit* 1.1.324–5)

> smooth <u>every passion</u>
> That in the natures of their Lords <u>rebel</u>   (F *KL* 2.2.72–3)

1.1.3   DELETION OF DETERMINERS: *THE, A/AN,* POSSESSIVES

Metrical considerations frequently license the deletion of a mono-syllabic determiner where retention would result in two weakly stressed function words coming together.

1.1.3a   Deletion of *the*

Type: Methought I sat in ^ seat of majesty
(Abbott, 89, 90)

The is often deleted in contexts such as

> Me thought I sate in ^ Seate of Majesty   (F *2H6* 1.2.36)

> And to ^ reliefe of Lazars, and weake age   (F *H5* 1.1.15)

> Forrage in ^ blood of ^ French Nobilitie   (F *H5* 1.2.110)

where the grammatical structure consists of two prepositional phrases (see section 1.4.1), one embedded in the other:

PP1(in ^ seat   PP2(of majesty))
PP1(to ^ relief   PP2(of lazars))
PP1(in ^ blood   PP2(of ^ French nobility))

The most likely explanation for this is metrical. Function words such as **prepositions** and the definite article are relatively unstressed when compared with **lexical nouns**. Retention of *the* in contexts such as these would tend to bring two weak stresses together:

w	w	s	w	s
<u>in</u>	<u>the</u>	seat	of	majesty

Deleting the article, however, produces two iambic feet, with function words in weakly stressed positions:

w	s	w	s
<u>in</u>	<u>seat</u>	of	majesty

Other such deletions can generally be explained by the same desire to avoid clusters of unstressed syllables. Abbott (82) associates *the* deletion with poetic archaism, citing

> Whereat, with blade, with bloody blamefull blade,
> He bravely broacht his boiling bloudy breast,
> And *Thisby*, tarrying in Mulberry shade,
> His dagger drew, and died
>
> (F *MND* 5.1.145–8)

and this hypothesis is supported by the frequency of *the* deletions in the early history plays.

The deletion is not obligatory, however. In the following two lines, note that deletion occurs only in the first line, despite a possible context for it in the second:

> I say, my Soveraigne, *Yorke* is ^ meetest man
> To be your Regent in <u>the</u> Realme of France
>
> (F *2H6* 1.3.160–1)

1.1.3b Deletion of possessive determiner

As with deletion of *the*, metrical considerations allow deletion of possessive determiners after a preposition to avoid runs of unstressed monosyllables:

> Not *Priamus*, and *Hecuba* on ^ knees
>
> (Q *TC* 5.3.54)

This avoids: 'Not Priamus, and Hecuba on <u>their</u> knees'.

1.1.3c Deletion of *a/an*

> Type: If ever I were ^ traitor
> (Abbott, 83–4, 86)

As with deletion of *the*, metrical considerations are probably most significant here. Interestingly, Abbott suggests that nouns without indefinite articles can be used in contrast with other nouns with the implication that the undetermined noun stands for a whole class:

Was ever ^ King that joy'd an earthly Throne,
And could command no more content then I?
No sooner was I crept out of my Cradle,
But I was made a King, at nine months olde.
Was never ^ Subject long'd to be a King,
As I do long and wish to be a Subject   (F *2H6* 4.9.1–6)

Here the apparent distinction between '^ Subject' at line 5 (that is, all subjects) and 'a Subject' at line 6 (that is, a particular subject) gives support to Abbott.

The following example makes Abbott's attempted distinction clear:

What a merit were it in death to take this poore
maid from the world? what ^ corruption in this life, that
it will let this man live?   (Fp *MM* 3.1.231–3)

where the merit is a specific one, and the corruption is seen to be general.

Compare this with other deletions of indefinite articles after *what*:

Cassius, what ^ Night is this?   (F *JC* 1.3.42)

That is, 'What kind of night is this?' – a general sense.

                    Ile tell the world aloud
What ^ man thou art   (F *MM* 2.4.152–3)

Jove knowes what ^ man thou might'st have made   (F *Cym* 4.2.207)

Deletion seems to be particularly likely after *ever/never*:

No *Bullingbroke*: if ever I were ^ Traitor   (F *R2* 1.3.201)

Those eyes, which never shed ^ remorsefull teare   (F *R3* 1.2.159)

                    Never ^ Master had
A Page so kinde   (F *Cym* 5.5.85–6)

Anthonio never yet was ^ Theefe, or ^ Pyrate   (F *TN* 5.1.72)

but is not obligatory:

I never saw a vessell of like sorrow   (F *WT* 3.3.21)

For never was a Storie of more Wo   (F *RJ* 5.3.309)

1.1.4 POSSESSION: 'GENITIVE' CONSTRUCTIONS

Type: a. *possessive pronoun*   thy eye
         b. s-*genitive*   Jove's lightning

c.	of *construction*	the jerks of invention
d.	*double genitive*	a sequent of the stranger Queen's
e.	*absolute genitive*	Your Ladyship's
f.	*zero genitive*	poor Clarence death
g.	his *genitive*	Mars his heart
h.	*split genitive*	the ladies hearts of France

Early Modern English had various means of expressing possession, most of which are associated with pre-head modification or determiners in some way (for example 'thy eye', 'Jove's lightning'). One highly frequent construction involves **post-head modification** ('the jerks of invention'), and therefore ought, strictly speaking, to be covered in section 1.4. However, because the field of meaning is conceptually coherent, and the histories of the various constructions are linked, I have gathered all of the relevant constructions together here, rather than have them scattered through the grammar.

In Old English, possession was marked by use of genitive **inflections** – and there were a wide range of possible endings depending on the type of noun involved: -*an* and -*a*, for example, as well as the -*es* which underlies modern -*s*. The general loss of inflections which occurred in late Old English and Middle English manifests itself in the case of the genitive with a spread of -*es* to almost all contexts, and the rise of an alternative prepositional construction for expressing possession. In the case of the genitive, both the inflected and the prepositional construction survive, so in Early Modern and Present-day English we have the following alternatives:

| Jove's lightning | vs | the lightning of Jove |
| the jerks of invention | vs | invention's jerks |

where the head noun (the thing possessed) is either pre-modified by a genitive noun phrase acting as a determiner:

| (Jove's) | lightning |
| *determiner* | *head* |

or is post-modified by a prepositional phrase:

| the | lightning | (of Jove) |
| *determiner* | *head* | *post-head modification* |

Note that the genitive noun phrase in the first example, like any other, is expandable:

| (the great god Jove's) | lightning |
| *determiner* | *head* |

These alternatives are, however, just the most frequent means of marking genitive relations in English. Some sense of the range of constructions available for expressing relationships of possession in Early Modern English can be gained from the following passage from *Love's Labour's Lost*. At this point in the play, Nathaniel (*Nath.*) and Holofernes (*Ped.* for Pedant, or *Hol.*) have intercepted a letter containing a love poem. The passage begins with Nathaniel reading the poem. The two men then discover its author, and indulge in some literary criticism. (Except for underlinings of possessive constructions, the passage is printed here as in the Folio: modern editions regularize the speech prefixes and reassign some speeches.)

> *Nath.* . . . [*reads*] If Love make me forsworne, how shall I sweare to love?
> Ah never faith could hold, if not to beautie vowed.
> Though to my selfe forsworn, to thee Ile faithfull prove.
> Those thoughts to mee were Okes, to thee like Osiers
>   bowed.
> Studie <u>his byas</u> leaves, and makes <u>his booke</u> <u>thine eyes</u>.   5
> Where all those pleasures live, that Art would compre-
>   hend.
> If knowledge be the marke, to know thee shall suffice.
> Well learned is that tongue, that well can thee comend.
> All ignorant that soule, that sees thee without wonder.   10
> Which is to me some praise, that I <u>thy parts</u> admire;
> <u>Thy eye *Ioves* lightning</u> beares, <u>thy voyce</u> <u>his dreadfull</u>
>   <u>thunder</u>.
> Which not to anger bent, is musique and sweet fire.
> Celestiall as thou art, Oh pardon love this wrong,   15
> That sings <u>heavens praise</u> with such an earthly tongue.
>
> *Ped.* You finde not the apostraphas, and so misse the accent. Let me supervise the cangenet.
>
> *Nath.* Here are onely numbers ratified, but for <u>the elegancy, facility, & golden cadence of poesie</u> *caret*: O-   20
> *viddius Naso* was the man. And why in deed *Naso*, but for smelling out <u>the odoriferous flowers of fancy</u>? <u>the jerkes of invention</u> imitarie is nothing: So doth the Hound <u>his master</u>, the Ape <u>his keeper</u>, the tyred Horse <u>his rider</u>: But *Damosella virgin*, Was this directed to   25
> you?
>
> *Iaq.* I sir from one mounsier *Berowne*, one of <u>the strange Queenes Lords</u>.
>
> *Nath.* I will overglance the superscript.

To the snow-white hand of the most beautious Lady Rosaline.   30
I will looke againe on the intellect of the Letter, for
the nomination of the partie written to the person written unto.
Your Ladiships in all desired imployment. Berowne.

  Per.   Sir *Holofernes*, this *Berowne* is one of the Votaries   35
with the King, and here he hath framed a Letter to a se-
quent of the stranger Queenes: which, accidentally, or
by the way of progression, hath miscarried. Trip and
goe, my sweete, deliver this Paper into the hand of the
King, it may concerne much: stay not thy complement, I   40
forgive thy duetie, adue.

  . . .

  Ped. . . . But to returne to the Verses, Did they please
you sir *Nathaniel*?

  Nath. Marveilous well for the pen.

  Peda. I do dine to day at the fathers of a certaine Pu-   45
pill of mine, where if (being repast) it shall please you to
gratifie the table with a Grace, I will on my priviledge I
have with the parents of the foresaid Childe or Pupill,
undertake *your bien vonuto*, where I will prove those
Verses to be very unlearned, neither savouring of   50
Poetrie, Wit, nor Invention. I beseech your So-
cietie.   (Fp *LLL*
4.2.101–38, 144–53)

The passage illustrates five of the different means of expressing possession in Early Modern English, detailed in sections 1.1.4a–e. Other
methods are discussed in the subsequent sections.

1.1.4a Possessive pronouns

The most straightforward method of marking possession is by using a
possessive pronoun as a determiner. This is also highly frequent, as the
three examples in the following line show:

  Studie his byas leaves, and makes his booke thine eyes

                                               (F *LLL* 4.2.109)

Note here the use of 'his' with the inanimate noun 'Studie'; Present-day
English would require 'its', but this pronoun **form** was rare in Early
Modern English – see section 1.3.2c.

1.1.4b s-genitive

The *s*-genitive derives from an Old English genitive ending, *-es*, which gradually replaced all other possible genitive endings during the Middle English period:

<u>*Ioves*</u> lightning   (F *LLL* 4.2.115)

<u>heavens</u> praise   (F *LLL* 4.2.118)

As the examples show, Present-day English orthographical conventions were not in place in the Early Modern period (see section 1.1.4i for comments on orthography).

1.1.4c *Of* construction

As Old English inflectional endings were lost from the language, their functions were often taken over by prepositional constructions. Genitive endings were replaced by the *of* construction:

the odoriferous flowers <u>of fancy</u>   (Fp *LLL* 4.2.124)

the jerkes <u>of invention</u>   (Fp *LLL* 4.2.124–5)

The inflectional *s*-genitive (1.1.4b) and the *of* construction are still in variation in Present-day English, though they are not necessarily synonymous (compare 'Laura<u>'s</u> painting' with 'a painting <u>of</u> Laura'). In Early Modern English, choice of one or other of the constructions can be affected by a variety of considerations. Metrics will clearly play a part in poetry. As this passage illustrates, animate nouns tend to favour *s*-genitives: here with 'Jove' and 'Queene'; but note inanimate '<u>heavens</u> praise'. Abstract or inanimate nouns tend to take the prepositional *of* construction: 'poesy', 'fancy', 'invention', 'letter'; but note that animate 'King' also takes *of*. Heavy pre-modification of the possessor may also favour *of*. Thus we have

the snow-white hand <u>of</u> the most beauteous Lady Rosaline

rather than

the most beauteous Lady Rosaline<u>'s</u> snow-white hand

Historically, the **analytic** *of* construction is more recent than its competitor, the Old English synthetic *s*-genitive, and the *of* construction may be modelled on similar structures in Romance languages. Holofernes' frequent use of the *of* construction here may suggest that it was considered more formal or pretentious (compare Present-day

English pairs such as 'Strathclyde University' and 'the University of Strathclyde').

1.1.4d Double genitive

In the double genitive, both the synthetic and analytic modes of marking possession are used:

> a sequent of the stranger <u>Queenes</u>   (Fp *LLL* 4.2.136–7)

This kind of **double marking** is common where two ways of forming a construction are in competition with each other. Compare this with 'the hand <u>of</u> the King' (139–40), where only the analytic construction is used.

1.1.4e Absolute genitive

In the absolute genitive, the genitive has the form of a determining genitive phrase, but acts as a head noun in its own right, rather than pre-modifying another noun:

> Your <u>Ladiships</u>   (Fp *LLL* 4.2.134)

Note how this construction can even take post-modification, as in the extraordinary

> <u>the fathers</u> of a certaine Pupill of mine   (Fp *LLL* 4.2.151–2)
> *head*   *post-head modification*

1.1.4f Zero genitive

Two of the possible Old English genitive inflections were zero and -*e*, and these may lie behind Early Modern zero genitives:

> my Unckle <u>*Clarence*</u> angry Ghost   (F *R3* 3.1.144)
>
> high you hence to Frier <u>*Lawrence*</u> Cell   (F *RJ* 2.5.69)
>
> for their owne <u>Credit</u> sake   (Fp *1H4* 2.1.71)
>
> at everie <u>sentence</u> end   (F *AYL* 3.2.133)

Phonotactic constraints are clearly also very important in triggering zero genitives. In these examples, zero is only found where the noun ends in [s] (so 'Clarence', 'Lawrence', 'sentence'), or where the following word begins with [s] (so 'Cell', 'sake'). Zero is not obligatory in such contexts however:

What is the Prince<u>s</u> Doome? (F *RJ* 3.3.4)

for Fame<u>s</u> sake (F *LLL* 4.1.32)

Nor is zero only found in these phonetic environments:

any <u>moment</u> leisure (F *Ham* 1.3.133)

The modern equivalent, 'any moment's leisure', appears in Q3. Similarly:

the <u>Region</u> Kites (F *Ham* 2.2.575)

The <u>region</u> cloude (Q *Son* 33.12)

his <u>heart</u> blood
Which breath'd this poyson (F *R2* 1.1.172)

1.1.4g *His* genitive

Incorrectly characterized as a mistake by Abbott (217), this construction can be found in Old English and in Middle English (similar constructions occur colloquially in German and Dutch). As these examples show, the construction favours proper names, especially those ending in [z]:

in a sea-fight 'gainst the Count <u>his</u> gallies (F *TN* 3.3.26)

Now where's the Bastards braves, and *Charles* <u>his</u> glikes?

(F *1H6* 3.2.123)

O, you my Lord, by *Mars* <u>his</u> gauntlet thanks (F *TC* 4.5.176)

Note the variation between 'Bastard<u>s</u> braves' and '*Charles* <u>his</u> glikes', where the [z] at the end of 'Charles' triggers the *his* genitive. Similar variation appears in *Henry V*:

So that, as cleare as is the Summers Sunne,
King *Pepins* Title, and *Hugh Capets* Clayme,
King *Lewes* <u>his</u> satisfaction, all appeare
To hold in Right and Title of the Female (F *H5* 1.2.86–9)

Other Early Modern writers have the construction with *her* and *their*. The contexts of use, and the high status of the individuals named (Mars, King Lewes), as well as its use in titles (for example Donne's *Ignatius His Conclave*) suggest that this construction may have formal stylistic weight.

1.1.4h Split genitive

The split construction is so called as the head noun 'splits' the elements of the modifying noun phrase.

> Me thinkes the Realmes of England, France, & Ireland,
> Beare that proportion to my flesh and blood,
> As did the fatall brand *Althœa* burnt,
> Unto <u>the Princes heart of *Calidon*</u>   (*2H6* 1.1.233–6)

> I tell thee *Poole*, when in the city *Tours*
> Thou ran'st a-tilt in honor of my Love,
> And stol'st away <u>the Ladies hearts of France</u>   (*2H6* 1.3.50–2)

In Present-day English these elements would have to be brought together into a 'group genitive':

split genitive	*group genitive*
the prince's heart of Calydon	the prince of Calydon's heart
the ladies hearts of France	the ladies of France's hearts

In the modern version, the genitive -*s* is attached to the end of a complex noun phrase ('<u>the ladies of France</u>'s', '<u>the prince of Calydon</u>'s') rather than appearing directly after the head. The group genitive was an innovation in Middle English, and it appears to have completely replaced the split construction by the end of the seventeenth century. Evidence for the marginality of the split construction, even in Early Modern English, may come from the way the Quarto of *2 Henry VI* (*The First Part of the Contention*) seems to avoid the second split construction at this point:

> I tell thee *Poull*, when thou didst runne at Tilt,
> And stolst away our Ladies hearts in *France*   (Q *2H6* 1.3.50–2)

The following is often cited as a split genitive:

> this same Scull sir, was Yoricks Scull, the Kings Jester   (Fp *Ham* 5.1.175)

but it may be more accurate to see this as an example of informal, speech-based syntax where **apposition** is being used.

1.1.4i Orthography

The Folio rarely uses apostrophes for genitive -*s*, tending to reserve them instead for **elisions** of the verb *to be*:

> The Aprill's in her eyes, it is Loves spring,
> And these the showers to bring it on   (F *AC* 3.2.43–4)

That is, 'The April <u>is</u> in her eyes, it is <u>Love's</u> spring'.
The Quartos tend to avoid apostrophes altogether:

> Wheres *Romeos* man?   (Q *RJ* 5.3.269)

The more formal Folio introduces a succession of distinctions in its printings of this line:

> Where's *Romeos* man?   (F cancel *RJ*)

> Where's *Romeo's* man?   (F reset *RJ*)

These two states can be seen in the second edition of the Norton Facsimile, edited by Peter Blayney, pages 916–17. The reset version's 'Romeo's' may be an anticipatory setting error, since 's genitives are so rare in the Folio elsewhere.

The possible variations in Early Modern orthography produce the multiple mind-bending ambiguities of *Loues labors lost* (as the title page of the Quarto has it), which can be modernized as

> Love's labour's lost   (The labour of love is lost)

> Love's labours lost   (Love is labours lost)

> Love's labours lost   (Love's labours (are) lost)

or even, given the possibility that 'labors' is a third person plural form (see section 2.1.8a):

> Loves labours lost   (Loves labour lost)

I am indebted to John Kerrigan's New Penguin edition (1982) of *Love's Labour's Lost* for this point (see page 147 for a discussion of the range of possible interpretations, which doesn't include my rather mischievous final suggestion).

PRE-HEAD ELEMENTS: MODIFICATION

1.2.0 OVERVIEW

Type:	*adjectival phrase*	a <u>fresh</u> admirer
	noun phrase	hunger-broke <u>stone</u> walls
	verb form	an <u>enforced</u> ceremony

Adjectival phrases are the items most frequently found as pre-head modification; for example:

a (<u>fresh</u>) Admirer   (F *H8* 1.1.3)

Your (<u>most grave</u>) Belly was deliberate   (F *Cor* 1.1.127)

Adjectival phrases are covered in sections 1.2.1–5.

   Noun phrases can also occur as pre-head modification. They do this when they occur in **apposition** with other noun phrases:

I am (<u>Cinna</u>) the Poet   (F *JC* 3.3.29)

(though note that we could just as reasonably regard 'the Poet' as *post*-head modification of 'Cinna' here!).

   Bare nouns can also function as adjectives:

Hunger-broke <u>stone</u> wals   (F *Cor* 1.1.205)

For such usages, see section 1.2.6.

   Many pre-modifying adjectives are formed from verbs:

an <u>enforced</u> Ceremony   (F *JC* 4.2.21)

these <u>Jigging</u> Fooles   (F *JC* 4.3.136)

These are covered in section 1.2.7.

   Other parts of speech functioning as adjectives are covered in section 1.2.8. More rarely, complex pre-modifying structures are found, such as:

<u>too hard a keeping</u> oth   (Q *LLL* 1.1.65)

the <u>alwaies winde-obeying</u> deepe (*CE* 1.1.63)

These are covered in section 1.2.9.

1.2.1 PLACEMENT OF ADJECTIVAL PHRASES

Type:	*attributive*	a <u>fresh</u> admirer
	postpositive	something <u>untimely</u>
	predicative	There's something in't / That is <u>deceivable</u>

There are three possible positions in the clause for adjectival phrases when they modify noun phrase heads. Often, the adjectival phrase will be located within the noun phrase, in either pre- or post-head position (see the first and second examples above), but a very frequent position for the adjectival phrase is outside the noun phrase it modifies, after the verb *to be* (as in the final example).

As with noun phrases (see section 1.0b), I use the term *adjectival phrase* rather than simple *adjective* because of the possibility of expansion:

a (very fresh) admirer
an ague (most untimely)
the admirer was (exceedingly fresh)

The three possible structural positions for modifying adjectival phrases have the following names:

1 **Attributive** – where the adjectival phrase appears within the noun phrase, pre-modifying the head noun:

a (<u>fresh</u>) Admirer (F *H8* 1.1.3)

An (<u>untimely</u>) Ague (F *H8* 1.1.4)

2 **Postpositive** – where the adjectival phrase appears within the noun phrase, post-modifying the head noun:

someone (<u>fresh</u>)
something (<u>untimely</u>)

3 **Predicative** – where the adjectival phrase appears after the verb as an independent element in clause structure:

the admirer was (<u>fresh</u>)
the ague was (<u>untimely</u>)

The three possible positions for adjectival modification give writers a range of stylistic and metrical options. Postpositive modification is the least common, and therefore is likely to place emphasis on the modification, rather than the thing modified (compare 'an untimely <u>ague</u>' with 'an ague <u>untimely</u>'). It is notably more frequent in verse than prose, and this has several possible explanations: it is **marked** for formality (being associated with Latinate and Romance structures); it allows words to be moved to fit the metrical template; it makes the modification more salient (desirable in figurative, self-consciously 'poetic' language).

Attributive and predicative modification are much less marked because they are more common. Again, though, they offer a stylistic distinction, since predicative structures tend to move the modifying adjective into a more *salient* position:

attributive   an <u>untimely</u> ague
predicative   the ague was <u>untimely</u>

Variation between these two types of modification in prose can indicate relative closeness to speech, since predicative constructions are most frequent in speech. Furthermore, prose uses predicative constructions to focus attention on the modification rather than the thing modified in the same way as verse uses postpositive constructions – without any increase in formality. See section 1.4.4 for more on postpositive adjectives.

1.2.2 ADJECTIVES: SCOPE

Type:
location of effect   a <u>fearful</u> man   vs   a <u>fearful</u> danger
subjectivization   their <u>awful</u> duty   vs   his <u>awful</u> essay
passivized   the <u>unexpressive</u> she   vs   the <u>unexpressible</u> she
(Abbott, 3, 4)

We tend to assume that an adjective refers to a quality inherent in the noun it modifies – in other words that its **scope** is relatively straightforward. For example:

a <u>fearful</u> man

is someone who feels fear – the scope of the adjective is the noun 'man'. However, adjectives can also refer to qualities or feelings the modified noun evokes in other entities:

a <u>fearful</u> danger

is not a danger which feels fear, but a danger which causes fear in others. In other words, the scope of the adjective goes beyond the phrase in which it appears to include an implicit other entity (in this case, the person who feels fear because of the danger).

Early Modern English shows considerable variation in the scope of adjectives, a field which Abbott covers using the terms *active* and *passive*. This is a complex area, full of fine semantic and conceptual distinctions, and it is not always easy to draw distinct lines between types of usage. I have identified three types of scope in Early Modern English adjectival use (as listed above): **location of effect**, **subjectivization** and **passivized**; and these are covered in sections 1.2.2a–c. After reading these sections, readers may not be entirely convinced that these *are* three distinct areas: this is a field where more detailed research is needed.

1.2.2a Location of effect

As stated above, adjectives can refer either to a quality inherent in the modified noun:

> a <u>fearful</u> man

where the fear is inherent in the man ('He is full of fear'); or to a quality the noun evokes in a second entity:

> a <u>fearful</u> danger

where the fear is not inherent in the danger, but is felt by the speaker ('The danger makes me feel full of fear'). I refer to this issue as *location of effect*.

Effect can either be **localized** on the modified noun, or **displaced** onto an implicit or explicit second party:

> To throw away the dearest thing he ow'd,
> As 'twere a <u>carelesse</u> Trifle   (F *Mac* 1.4.10–11)

That is, 'the trifle is something *of which he is* careless' – the adjective 'careless' has the displaced sense, referring to a quality felt by a second party, not inherent in the noun modified (the trifle is not itself careless!).

In some cases usage can be ambiguous:

> Heavens Cherubin, hors'd
> Upon the <u>sightlesse</u> Curriors of the Ayre   (F *Mac* 1.7.22–3)

Here, 'the <u>sightlesse</u> Curriors of the Ayre' are the winds. I take 'sightlesse' to carry the displaced sense of 'invisible' ('they are unseen by me'), rather than the localized sense of 'blind' ('the winds are unable to see'). Compare this with a more expected localized usage of 'sightless' in the *Sonnets*:

> my drooping eye-lids open wide,
> Looking on darknes which the blind doe see.
> Save that my soules imaginary sight
> Presents (thy) shaddoe to my <u>sightles</u> view   (Q *Son* 27.7–10)

In *King Lear*, 'comfortable' is used unexpectedly in a displaced sense twice, once with predicative position:

> I have another daughter,
> Who I am sure is kinde and <u>comfortable</u>   (F *KL* 1.4.303–4)

> Approach thou Beacon to this under Globe,
> That by thy <u>comfortable</u> Beames I may
> Peruse this Letter   (F *KL* 2.2.161–3)

Here, on both occasions, 'comfortable' means 'giving comfort to someone else', rather than the only possible modern sense, which is the localized 'being in a state of comfort'.

Other *-able* adjectives used with displaced effect include:

> Shew me thy humble heart, and not thy knee,
> Whose dutie is <u>deceivable</u>, and false   (F *R2* 2.3.84–5)

> there's something in't
> That is <u>deceiveable</u>   (F *TN* 4.3.20–1)

Here the sense is the displaced one of 'deceptive of others', not the localized 'something in it which makes it liable to being deceived'.

Similarly with the use of 'contemptible' in the following:

> 'tis very possible hee'l scorne it, for the man (as you
> know all) hath a contemptible spirit   (Fp *MA* 2.3.175–6)

Here, 'contemptible' carries the displaced sense 'a spirit prone to hold others in contempt', not the localized 'a spirit to be held in contempt'. Adjectives formed with the *-able/-ible* suffix are now always localized, but in Early Modern English they could carry displaced meanings.

Further examples:

> At *Ephesus* the Temple see,
> Our King and all his companie.
> That he can hither come so soone,
> Is by your fancies <u>thankful</u> doome   (Q *Per* 5.2.17–20)

That is, 'I am thankful that the judgement ('doom') of your imagina-tions ('fancies') allows the king to make this journey'. In other words, the doom is deserving of thanks (displaced), rather than giving thanks (localized).

> We Hermia, like two <u>Artificiall</u> gods,
> Have with our needles, created both one flower   (F *MND* 3.2.203–4)

That is, 'gods who can make things' (displaced), rather than the local-ized 'gods who have been made'.

> Loe, in these windowes that let forth thy life,
> I powre the <u>helplesse</u> Balme of my poore eyes   (F *R3* 1.2.12–13)

The balm is unhelpful/useless to others (displaced) – not the modern, localized sense of 'unable to help itself'.

Abbott includes the following examples in his paragraph 4, under the rubric of 'cause for effect', but they seem to me to be examples of a shift in location of effect again:

> There is an old poore man,
> Who after me, hath many a weary steppe
> Limpt in pure love: till he be first suffic'd,
> Opprest with two <u>weake</u> evils, age, and hunger,
> I will not touch a bit   (F *AYL* 2.7.129–33)

Here the 'two weake evils' are not in themselves weak (localized sense), but they produce weakness in the person they affect (displaced). Similarly:

> Sixt part of each?
> A <u>trembling</u> Contribution   (F *H8* 1.2.94–5)

where the contribution is so great as to induce trembling in those it is expected from (displaced sense).

Futurity (prolepsis)

Related to shifts in location of effect, this is a specialized usage of adjec-tives whereby an effect which *will be* produced is represented as already *having been* produced:

> Heere shall they make their ransome on the sand,
> Or with their blood staine this <u>discoloured</u> shore   (F *2H6* 4.1.10–11)

where the shore, which *will* be stained red if their blood is spilled, is already imagined as 'discoloured'. Similarly:

> go on;
> Be as a Planetary plague, when Jove
> Will o're some high-Vic'd City hang his poyson
> In the <u>sicke</u> ayre   (F *Tim* 4.3.109–12)

where the air, which *will* be poisoned by Jove, is already imagined as 'sick'.

1.2.2b Subjectivization

Subjectivization is the term for a particular kind of shift in sense which has occurred in many adjectives. The shift involves a move from describing an objective quality inherent in the modified noun, to carrying the subjective impression of the speaker. For example, in Present-day English 'an awful team' is a team I do not rate very highly: the adjective carries my subjective impression of the team. Originally, however, 'awful' carried the sense 'filled with religious awe', and could only have been used to describe a team which was objectively feeling awe. Today, 'a sad man' can mean either 'a man who feels sadness' (inherent, objective quality), or 'a man I think is uncool' (subjective impression).

Frequently in Early Modern English we find adjectives used in their pre-subjectivized state, where today they can only be used in a subjectivized sense:

> how dare thy joynts forget
> To pay their <u>awfull</u> dutie to our presence?   (F *R2* 3.3.75–6)

That is, the duty is full of awe – not, as modern usage would have it, done badly!

> *Glou.*   What Paper were you reading?
> *Bast.*   Nothing my Lord.
> *Glou.*   No? What needed then that <u>terrible</u> dispatch of
> it into your Pocket? The quality of nothing, hath not
> such neede to hide it selfe   (Fp *KL* 1.2.30–4)

Here, Gloucester suggests that Edmund's ('*Bast.*') hurried movements to hide a letter he was reading were motivated by terror – that they are literally 'terrible' or 'full of terror'. The subjectivized modern sense would be that Gloucester thought Edmund had fumbled and put the letter away clumsily. Similarly:

> This to me
> In <u>dreadfull</u> secrecie impart they did   (F *Ham* 1.2.206–7)

Where 'dreadfull' carries an objective rather than subjectivized sense:
the secrecy was laden with dread.

> Come, let me clutch thee:
> I have thee not, and yet I see thee still.
> Art thou not fatal Vision, <u>sensible</u>
> To feeling, as to sight?   (F *Mac* 2.1.34–7)

Here Macbeth addresses his vision of a dagger, using 'sensible' in an
objective sense meaning 'able to be felt', rather than the more usual
current meaning, the highly subjectivized 'something I deem reason-
able'. Hamlet too uses 'sensible' objectively:

> Before my God, I might not this beleeve
> Without the <u>sensible</u> and true avouch
> Of mine owne eyes   (F *Ham* 1.1.59–61)

Similarly:

> It cannot be but he was murdred heere,
> The least of all these signes were <u>probable</u>   (F *2H6* 3.2.176–7)

Where 'probable' means 'would give objective proof' – not the subjectivized, modern sense of 'would seem to me to be likely'.

Subjectivized uses do exist in Early Modern English though:

> Halfe way downe
> Hangs one that gathers Sampire: <u>dreadfull</u> Trade   (F *KL* 4.6.14–15)

Trades can hardly feel dread – so 'dreadful' must carry Edgar's displaced
subjective opinion of the trade – the feeling it evokes in him, rather
than expressing some inherent quality of the trade. 'Dreadful' crops up
again in this sense in *Hamlet*:

> What if it tempt you toward the Floud my Lord?
> Or to the <u>dreadfull</u> Sonnet of the Cliffe,
> That beetles o're his base into the Sea   (F *Ham* 1.4.69–71)

The dread is in the mind of the speaker, rather than being an inherent
quality of the clifftop. The Folio's 'Sonnet of the Cliffe' is usually modernized to 'summit of the cliff', with editors assuming a minim error for
Q2's 'somnet', a possible Early Modern spelling of 'summit'. However,
it seems a shame to lose such a good joke, just for the sake of being
right, and 'dreadful sonnet' gives another subjectivized use of 'dreadful', however accidental.

1.2.2c Passivized

Some adjectives, especially ones derived with **negative particles** such as *un-*, crop up in senses which can best be paraphrased using **passive** constructions:

> Your love deserves my thanks, but my desert
> Unmeritable, shunnes your high request   (F *R3* 3.7.153–4)

where 'Unmeritable' can be glossed as 'unable to be rewarded'. Similarly:

> This is a slight unmeritable man,
> Meet to be sent on Errands   (F *JC* 4.1.12–13)

and

> A bawbling Vessel was he Captaine of,
> For shallow draught and bulke unprizable   (F *TN* 5.1.52–3)

That is, 'not worth making a prize of'.

In Present-day English, adjectives formed with *-able* always have a passive sense, while those formed with *-ive* are **active**; for example:

expandable   something which can be expanded
expansive   something which extends over a large area

In the Early Modern period however, *-ive* could appear in passive contexts:

>   do not staine
> The even vertue of our Enterprize,
> Nor th'insuppressive Mettle of our Spirits,
> To thinke, that or our Cause, or our performance
> Did neede an Oath   (F *JC* 2.1.132–6)

where 'insuppressive' means 'unsurpressable' or 'not able to be supressed'. Similarly:

> The providence that's in a watchful State,
> Knowes almost every graine of Plutoes gold;
> Findes bottome in th'uncomprehensive deepes   (F *TC* 3.3.195–7)

That is, 'unknowable'. The adjective 'uncomprehensive' today would imply the active sense 'unknowing'. And:

> Run, run *Orlando*, carve on every Tree,
> The faire, the chaste, and unexpressive shee   (F *AYL* 3.2.9–10)

Here 'unexpressive' does not mean 'silent', as modern usage would lead us to expect, but 'unable to be expressed'.

Note the *active* use of the following adjective formed with *-able*:

I have derision <u>medicinable</u>,
To use betweene your strangenesse and his pride   (F *TC* 3.3.44–5)

Here 'medicinable' has the sense 'able to act as a medicine', not the passive sense 'able to be treated'.

1.2.3 ADJECTIVES: COMPARATIVE AND SUPERLATIVE

Type: sweet   sweeter   sweetest
          unkind   more unkind   most unkind
          unkind   more unkinder   most unkindest
(Abbott, 6–11, 17)

Adjectives are gradable by the use of **comparative** and superlative forms:

sweete Clowne,
sweet<u>er</u> Foole, sweet<u>est</u> Lady   (Qp *LLL* 4.3.15–16)

Such forms can appear predicatively as well as attributively (see section 1.2.1):

I do affect the verie ground (which is <u>base</u>) where her shoo (which is <u>baser</u>) guided by her foote (which is <u>basest</u>) doth tread.   (Qp *LLL* 1.2.160–2)

The inflectional comparative (*-er*) and superlative (*-est*) endings function **synthetically**, but English also maintains an **analytic** means of marking these features by *more* and *most*:

synthetic		*analytic*
sweet<u>er</u>	vs	<u>more</u> sweet
sweet<u>est</u>	vs	<u>most</u> sweet

In Present-day Standard English, adjectives are usually restricted to one of the two methods of forming comparisons. Monosyllabic adjectives are generally synthetic:

red   redder   reddest
        ?more red   ?most red

while polysyllabic adjectives tend to be analytic:

horrible	*horribler	*horriblest
	more horrible	most horrible

Early Modern English, however, shows greater tolerance for adding inflections to polysyllabic adjectives:

> A Jewell lockt into the <u>wofulst</u> Caske,
> That ever did containe a thing of worth   (F *2H6* 3.2.409–10)

That is, 'the most woeful cask'.

Double marking

Very frequently Early Modern English shows both analytic and synthetic marking on the same adjective for emphasis, in the so-called *double comparative* form:

> opinion, a more
> soveraigne Mistris of Effects, throwes a <u>more safer</u>
> voice on you   (Fp *Oth* 1.3.224–6)

Analytic and synthetic forms also co-occur in superlative constructions:

> This was the <u>most unkindest</u> cut of all   (F *JC* 3.2.181)

> the <u>most boldest</u> and best hearts of Rome   (F *JC* 3.1.121)

Such forms were rigorously proscribed out of the written language in the eighteenth century, but remain in spoken English. They do not carry the connotations of informality or lack of education in Early Modern usage that they do today.

Early Modern English also allows the addition of comparative inflections to words such as 'worse', which were taken to be inherently comparative by prescriptivists:

> [*Iago.*]   How do you now, lieutenant?
> *Cas.*   The <u>worser</u>, that you give me the addition
> Whose want even killes me   (F *Oth* 4.1.104–6)

and

> *Rod.*   My name is *Rodorigo*.
> *Bra.*   The <u>worsser</u> welcome   (Fp *Oth* 1.1.93–4)

However, at this point the Quarto prints

> *Rod.* My name is *Roderigo.*
> *Bra.* The <u>worse</u> welcome (Qp *Oth* 1.1.93–4)

This indicates that Early Modern speakers tolerated a degree of variation between the forms; and it is significant that those preparing the more prestigious Folio edition did not regard 'worsser' as stigmatized.

The two texts of *Othello* show interesting variation in the use of adjectival forms such as these. Generally, the Folio text has forms which we would not regard as standard today:

> The worsser (F *Oth* 1.1.94)
>
> more safer (Fp *Oth* 1.3.225)
>
> The worser (F *Oth* 4.1.104)
>
> more neerer (F *Oth* 5.2.109)

while the Quarto text sometimes has the more standard version, and sometimes has the non-standard version:

> The worse (Q *Oth* 1.1.94)
>
> more safer (Qp *Oth* 1.3.225)
>
> The worser (Q *Oth* 4.1.104)
>
> more neere (Q *Oth* 5.2.109)

1.2.4 ADJECTIVAL INFLECTIONS

> Type: hempen
> brazen
> twiggen

In keeping with the general loss of inflections in English, almost all adjectives had lost the possibility of taking inflectional endings (other than the comparative ones – see 1.2.3) by the Middle English period. However, some adjectives denoting the substance of which a thing is composed retain an *-en* suffix to the present day: gold<u>en</u>, wood<u>en</u>, wooll<u>en</u>, earth<u>en</u>, for example. In Present-day English, these exist alongside uninflected variants:

> a gold ring   vs   a gold<u>en</u> ring
> a wool jumper   vs   a wooll<u>en</u> jumper

and the inflected variant often carries archaic or formal connotations. Similar variations occur in Early Modern English:

That Booke in manies eyes doth share the glorie,
That in <u>Gold</u> claspes, Locks in the <u>Golden</u> storie   (F *RJ* 1.3.91–2)

The relationship between the inflected and uninflected variants is not the same as in Present-day English however. The *OED* (*-en*, *suffix*[4]) notes the long survival of adjectival *-en* in south-west dialects of English, and Shakespeare's preference is overwhelmingly for inflected forms:

	inflected	*uninflected*
golden/gold	105	4
leaden/lead	18	0
silken/silk	17	4
brazen/bronze	13	0
wooden/wood	9	0
waxen/wax	8	0
hempen/hemp	3	0

Shakespeare's few uninflected uses of 'gold' as an adjective are instructive:

his <u>gold</u> complexion   (Q *Son* 18.6)

those <u>gould</u> candells fixt in heavens ayer   (Q *Son* 21.12)

The Cowslips tall, her pensioners bee;
In their <u>gold</u> coats, spots you see   (F *MND* 2.1.10–11)

That Booke in manies eyes doth share the glorie,
That in <u>Gold</u> claspes, Locks in the Golden storie   (F *RJ* 1.3.91–2)

Every one comes in rhymed verse (though none is used for rhyme), suggesting that Shakespeare only uses uninflected 'gold' when metrical considerations force him to. The example from *Romeo and Juliet* may also illustrate a stylistic difference: uninflected 'Gold' used for the metal, while 'Golden' is used for the more metaphorical sense.

The uninflected forms of 'silk' seem less clearly motivated, perhaps because 'golden' was **lexicalized** as a poeticism, and so harder to avoid:

a <u>silk</u> button   (F *RJ* 2.4.23)

Her Inkle, <u>Silke</u>   (Q *Per* 5.0.8)
(i.e. 'her thread, made of silk')

<u>Silk</u> stockings   (Fp *2H4* 2.2.14)

your blacke <u>silke</u> haire   (F *AYL* 3.5.46)

Shakespeare's preference for -*en* forms results in a wide range of adjectives with the inflection:

> Ye shall have a <u>hempen</u> Ca[u]dle then, & the help
> of hatchet　　　　　　　　　　　　　　　　　　(Fp *2H6* 4.7.85–6)

That is, 'You shall have a drink of rope (be hanged) and then be beheaded'.

> Well said, <u>Brazon</u>-face　　　　　　　　　　(Fp *MW* 4.2.124)

> O you <u>leaden</u> messengers　　　　　　　　　(F *AW* 3.2.108)

> The Pedlers <u>silken</u> Treasury　　　　　　　　(F *WT* 4.4.351)

> For men have marble, women <u>waxen</u> mindes　　(Q *Luc* 1240)

> a <u>Twiggen</u>-Bottle　　　　　　　　　　　　(Fp *Oth* 2.3.141)

A 'Twiggen' bottle is a bottle made of twigs – this phrase appears as 'a wicker bottle' in the Quarto.

> I combat challenge of this <u>Latine</u> Bilboe　　(Fp *MW* 1.1.146)

Here Pistol compares Slender to a stage-prop sword ('Bilboe') made of wood (lath – hence 'Latine' or latten). The fact that Pistol's **idiolect** is almost always archaic and pompous (evidenced here by the inversion of 'I combat challenge') may suggest that the inflected adjective is beginning to carry archaic connotations at this time too. A similar reference to the morality play character of Vice in *Twelfth Night* avoids the inflected form (though clearly rhyme is involved in the choice of construction):

> Who with dagger <u>of lath</u>, in his rage and his wrath,
> 　　　cries ah ha, to the divell　　　　　　(F *TN* 4.2.129–30)

This final instance is a useful reminder that the real competition in Shakespeare is not between inflected and uninflected forms of the adjective (since uninflected forms are virtually absent), but between inflected adjectives, and prepositional phrases which retain the original *noun* in a post-modifying phrase:

> The singing Masons building roofes <u>of Gold</u>　(F *H5* 1.2.198)

> 　　　Since you have shore
> With sheeres, his thred <u>of silke</u>　　　　　(F *MND* 5.1.327–8)

Non-adjectival -*en* inflections

Adjectival -*en* forms need to be distinguished from various other forms ending in *-en*, some of which can also be used as adjectives. Most frequent are adjectives derived from past participles ending in *-en*:

| when thou art dead and <u>rotten</u> | (Fp *WT* 3.3.81) |

| *as white as <u>driven</u> Snow* | (F *WT* 4.4.220) |

| I make a <u>broken</u> deliverie of the Businesse | (Fp *WT* 5.2.9) |

Nouns inflected with the diminutive *-en* are also used as adjectives:

| the <u>maiden</u> burning of his cheekes | (Q *VA* 50) |

Nouns carrying *-en* plural marking (e.g. 'children') and *-en* feminine marking (e.g. 'vixen') tend not to occur as adjectives.

1.2.5 ADJECTIVES: COMPOUND ADJECTIVES

Type: sudden-bold
         silly-stately
(Abbott, 2)

Shakespeare often joins two adjectives in a compound, with the first (as Abbott notes) acting as an **adverb** to modify the first. Present-day English would require the first element of the following compounds to carry an adverbial inflection:

| I am too <u>sodaine bold</u> | (F *LLL* 2.1.106) |

which would appear in Present-day English as

I am too sudden<u>ly</u> bold

It is important to note that neither Quarto nor Folio texts hyphenate these 'compounds': sometimes they have a comma between them, more commonly a space. Both conventions can be found in the same line for 'active-valiant' and 'valiant-young' in the First Folio (and the Quarto) text of *1 Henry IV*:

I do not thinke a braver Gentleman,	
More active, valiant, or more valiant yong,	
More daring, or more bold, is now alive	(F *1H4* 5.1.90)

The following will give a sense of the variation in punctuation:

| daring hardy | (Q *R2* 1.3.43) |

| daring, hardie | (F *R2* 1.3.43) |

Honorable dangerous	(F *JC* 1.3.124)
crafty sick	(Q and F *2H4* Induction 37)
I am too childish, foolish for this world	(Q *R3* 1.3.142)
I am too childish foolish for this World	(F *R3* 1.3.142)
You are too senselesse obstinate, my Lord,	(F *R3* 3.1.44)
Heere's a silly stately stile indeede	(F *1H6* 4.7.72)

Apparently uniquely, 'fertile-fresh' is hyphenated in F *Merry Wives*:

Mo[r]e fertile-fresh	(F *MW* 5.5.69)

It is worth noting that these compounds almost always occur in predicative position (after the verb, rather than inside the noun phrase as pre-head modification). This is probably because they are unusual, and therefore likely to require careful processing.

1.2.6 NOUNS AS PRE-MODIFIERS

Type: <u>stone</u> jugs
the <u>region</u> kites
his <u>music</u> vows

(Abbott, 22, 430)

As in Present-day English, Early Modern English frequently has nouns as pre-modifiers:

she brought <u>stone</u> Jugs	(F *TS* 0.2.89)
<u>heart</u>-greefe	(F *H5* 2.2.27)

As might be expected, given the general character of Early Modern English, this tendency goes even further in Early Modern usage, with bare nouns appearing where Present-day English would require a pre-modifying genitive phrase:

any <u>moment</u> leisure	(F *Ham* 1.3.133)

The modern equivalent, 'any moment's leisure', appears in Q3. Similarly:

the <u>Region</u> Kites	(F *Ham* 2.2.575)
The <u>region</u> cloude	(Q *Son* 33.12)

his <u>heart</u> blood

Which breath'd this poyson   (F *R2* 1.1.172)

Bare nouns also appear in contexts where Present-day English would require the adjectival ending *-al*:

the Honie of his <u>Musicke</u> Vowes   (F *Ham* 3.1.158)

and also *-ous*:

Todes infect faire founts with <u>venome</u> mud   (Q *Luc* 850)

The <u>venome</u> clamors of a jealous woman   (F *CE* 5.1.69)

Shakespeare is also happy to use proper names as modifiers where Present-day English would probably prefer either a genitive phrase or an *of* construction:

silence like a <u>Lucresse</u> knife   (F *TN* 2.5.107)

That is, 'silence, like Lucretia's knife'. Also:

here in <u>Philippi fields</u>   (F *JC* 5.5.19)

Compare this with 'the fields of Philippi'.

There is no world without *<u>Verona</u>* <u>walles</u>   (F *RJ* 3.3.17)

Present-day: 'Verona's walls' or 'the walls of Verona'. And:

To the <u>Cyprus Warres</u>   (F *Oth* 1.1.150)

From *<u>Leonati</u>* <u>Seate</u>   (F *Cym* 5.4.60)

1.2.7 VERB FORMS AS PRE-MODIFIERS

Type: *-ing* form   a <u>rising</u> sigh
          -en form   My thrice-<u>driven</u> bed of down
                          a well-<u>graced</u> actor

As in Present-day English, verb forms derived from present and past participles (here termed **-ing** and **-en forms** – see section 2.1.4) are frequently found in pre-modifying structures. Although derived from verbal forms, these words behave like adjectives in such contexts:

with a <u>rising</u> sigh,

He wisheth you in Heaven   (F *1H4* 3.1.8–9)

Note that the term '*-en* forms' derives from those past participles which are formed with an *-en* ending (such as *give/given, drive/driven, hide/hidden*), but it also covers past participles formed with *-ed* (*walk/walked*), and irregular participles (*come/come*):

My thrice-<u>driven</u> bed of Downe	(F *Oth* 1.3.231)
a well <u>grac'd</u> Actor	(F *R2* 5.2.24)
the new-<u>made</u> King	(F *R2* 5.2.45)
the new-<u>come</u> Spring	(F *R2* 5.2.47)

Holofernes gives a list of *-en* forms functioning as adjectives in his description of Dull's country manners:

> to show as it were
> his inclination after his undressed, unpolished, uneducated, unpruned, untrained, or rather unlettered, or ratherest, unconfirmed fashion   (Fp *LLL* 4.2.15–18)

1.2.8 OTHER PARTS OF SPEECH AS PRE-MODIFIERS (CONVERSION)

Shakespeare's frequent use of **conversion** (sometimes less clearly but more impressively termed **zero-morpheme derivation**) means that almost any part of speech can turn up performing the function of one of the others. In addition to the pre-modifiers noted above, it is possible to find prepositions, adverbs and non-participial verbs functioning as adjectives:

Prepositions

each <u>under</u> eye	(Q *Son* 7.2)
this <u>beneath</u> world	(F *Tim* 1.1.44)

Adverbs

the fine point of <u>seldome</u> pleasure	(Q *Son* 52.4)
But I (of thee) will wrest an Alphabet, And by <u>still</u> practice, learne to know thy meaning	(F *Tit* 3.2.44–5)
But that <u>still</u> use of greefe, makes wilde greefe tame, My tongue should to thy eares not name my Boyes	(F *R3* 4.4.230–1)

Verbs

As <u>hush</u> as death   (F *Ham* 2.2.482)

So much I hate a <u>breaking</u> cause to be
Of heavenly oaths   (F *LLL* 5.2.355–6)

1.2.9 COMPLEX PRE-MODIFYING STRUCTURES

Rarely, complex structures can be found in pre-modifying position. These are usually clauses (though not always), and can typically be paraphrased into more expected post-head modifying relative clauses:

The <u>nere-yet beaten</u> Horse of Parthia   (F *AC* 3.1.33)

having sworne <u>too hard a keeping</u> oath   (F *LLL* 1.1.65)

the <u>alwaies winde-obeying</u> deepe   (F *CE* 1.1.63)

spight of <u>cormorant devouring Time</u>   (F *LLL* 1.1.4)

Here, the first example involves an *adverbial* + *past-participle* construction, and could be paraphrased 'The horse of Parthia, which have never yet been beaten'. The second and third examples are based around **present participles**, and could be paraphrased respectively 'an oath which is too hard to keep' and 'the deep, which always obeys the wind'.

The final example is ambiguous, though the most likely analysis has the pre-modifying structure as two adjectives in apposition, paraphrasable as 'Time, which devours like a cormorant'. It can also be read, however, as a *noun* + *present participle* construction, with the sense 'Time, which devours even the greedy cormorant'.

A general point to arise from this is shown by comparing the originals with their post-modifying paraphrases: pre-modification is more concentrated, more metaphorical (because less explicit), and also more ambiguous and difficult to process; post-head modification is more explicit, more measured – and less risky.

THE HEAD

1.3.0 OVERVIEW

Noun phrases must contain a *head*. Most frequently this will be a *noun* or *pronoun*, but occasionally it can be an *adjective* or *determiner*. The heads of noun phrases can be identified by three tests:

1 They cannot be deleted.

2 They can usually be replaced by a pronoun.

3 They can usually be made plural or singular (this may not be possible with proper names).

Only test 1 holds good for all heads: the results for 2 and 3 depend on the type of head.

Examples of the tests

Nouns as heads (noun phrases are bracketed, heads are underlined):

(Mine <u>Eyes</u>) are full of (<u>Teares</u>)   (F *R2* 4.1.244)

1 *(Mine ____) are full of (____)
   'Eyes' and 'Teares' cannot be deleted

2 (<u>They</u>) are full of (<u>them</u>)
   'Eyes' and 'Teares' can be replaced by pronouns

3 (My <u>eye</u>) is full of (a <u>tear</u>)
   'Eyes' and 'Teares' can be made singular

Note that these tests can also be used to show which of two apparent noun heads is the actual one. In the following example, 'stone' and 'Jugs' look as though they could both be noun heads:

Because she brought stone Jugs, and no seal'd quarts

(F *TS* Induction.2.89)

But test 3 shows that 'Jugs' must be the head, with 'stone' acting as pre-head modification:

> 3 *Because she brought (<u>stones</u> jugs) and no seal'd quarts
> 'stone' cannot be made plural
>
> Because she brought (a stone <u>jug</u>) and no seal'd quarts
> 'Jugs' can be made singular

Pronouns as heads

(I) knew (you) at the first   (F *TS* 2.1.196)

1 *(_) knew (___) at the first
neither 'I' nor 'you' can be deleted

2 not applicable

3 (<u>We</u>) knew (<u>you</u>) at the first
both 'I' and 'you' can be made plural

Adjectives as heads

the bottome of (the deepe)   (F *1H4* 1.3.201)

1 *the bottome of (the ___)
'deep' cannot be deleted

2 the bottome of (<u>it</u>)
'deep' can be replaced by a pronoun

3 the bottome of (the <u>deeps</u>)
'deep' can be made plural

And similarly:

(Small) have continuall plodders ever wonne   (F *LLL* 1.1.86)
which passes tests 1 and 2:

1 *(___) have continual plodders ever won

2 (<u>This</u>) have continual plodders ever won

Determiners as heads

I knew you at (the first)   (F *TS* 2.1.196)

1 *I knew you at (the ____)
'first' cannot be deleted

2 I knew you at (<u>it</u>)
'first' can be replaced by a pronoun

3 *?I knew you at (the firsts)
   'first' cannot be made plural?

Frequently, adjective and determiner heads can be assumed to be the product of **ellipsis** of a noun – for example:

The bottom of (the deep <u>ocean</u>)
I knew you at (the first <u>sight</u>)

but the possibility of pluralization (e.g. 'deeps') shows that adjectives especially can be analysed as full heads.

Generally, Early Modern nouns behave identically to Present-day nouns in respect to these tests. The only major differences are in the case of plural inflections, where some variation can be found (see section 1.3.1).

Early Modern pronouns also behave identically to their Present-day equivalents in respect to these tests, but there are considerable differences in form and function between Early Modern and Present-day pronouns which will be analysed in depth in section 1.3.2.

1.3.1 NOUNS: PLURAL INFLECTIONS

Type: shoes/shoon
       eyes/eyne
       sheep/sheeps

Old English nouns were made plural by the addition of one of a number of different inflections. During the Middle English period, in a process known as **levelling**, one of the possible plural inflections (-s) steadily took over from the others, bringing about the Present-day situation where -s is almost the only means of marking plurality. The few exceptions include some borrowings from Latin and Greek (which tend to have -s plural alternates as well, for example *stadia/stadiums*), and a very few survivals of the lost Old English inflections:

zero	deer	sheep	fish
-en	oxen	brethren	

Chicken was originally the plural of *chick*, but at some point was reanalysed as a singular form, so now gets a second plural marker added for plural inflection: *chick-en-s*.

Some Old English plural forms survive in Shakespeare. However, they are restricted to rhymes or deliberate archaisms. None seem to be **unmarked**:

> Spare none but such as go in clouted <u>shooen</u>   (F 2H6 4.3.174)

That is, 'shoes'.

> *How should I your true love know from another one?*
> *By his Cockle hat and staffe and his Sandal <u>shoone</u>*   (F Ham 4.5.23–6)

The first instance here is probably intended as a marker of Jack Cade's rebels' low, rustic status; the *Hamlet* example comes from one of Ophelia's distracted songs. These are the only examples of *shoon* in Shakespeare, against twenty-one of *shoes*.

Similarly marked in usage is the *-en* plural of 'eye':

> Alas, he naught esteems that face of thine,
> To which loves eyes paies tributarie gazes,
> Nor thy soft handes, sweet lips, and crystall <u>eine</u>   (Q VA 631–3)

used solely for rhyme here, as shown by the use of modern 'eyes' at line 632. Rhyme uses of *eyne* are relatively frequent in Shakespeare:

> *If the scorne of your bright <u>eine</u>*
> *Have power to raise such love in mine*   (F AYL 4.3.50–1)

> Here's *Lucentio*, right sonne to the right *Vin-*
> *centio*,
> That have by marriage made thy daughter mine,
> While counterfeit supposes bleer'd thine <u>eine</u>   (F TS 5.1.104–7)

> Oft did she heave her Napkin to her <u>eyne</u>,
> Which on it had conceited characters:
> Laundring the silken figures in the brine   (Q LC 15–16)

> O *Helen*, goddesse, nimph, perfect, divine,
> To what my love, shall I compare thine <u>eyne</u>   (F MND 3.2.137–8)

Non-rhyme usages always have some indication that the form is a deliberate archaism. For example, 'eyne' collocates with the archaic form 'gan' in *Lucrece*:

> Even so the maid with swelling drops gan wet
> Her circled <u>eien</u> inforst, by simpathie   (Q Luc 1228–9)

and appears in one of Gower's choruses in *Pericles*:

> The Catte with <u>eyne</u> of burning cole,
> Now coutches from the Mouses hole   (Q Per 3.0.5–6)

Shakespeare uses *eyne* twelve times in total: ten times in poetry for rhyme, twice for archaic effect. He uses *eyes* 706 times in all contexts.

Some variation in plural marking survives into Present-day English (it is possible to find both *fish* and *fishes* as plural forms, for example), and Shakespeare shows variation between zero and *-s* forms. There is one instance of *sheeps*, rather than the expected *sheep*:

Two hot Sheepes   (F *LLL* 2.1.218)

Spoken by Katherine (a high-status character), the form is used to generate a pun with 'ships'.

There is more extensive variation between *fish* and *fishes* (8 versus 11 instances by my count), and it is difficult to identify any semantic pattern behind the variation. In Present-day usage the two forms of the plural are often associated with **count** (*fishes*) and **non-count** (*fish*) usages of nouns:

I caught seven fishes   (count)
All the fish in the sea   (non-count)

It seems more likely that Shakespearean variation is patterned by metrical considerations, as the successive uses of 'fish' and 'fishes' in the following passage indicate:

The beasts, the <u>fishes</u>, and the winged fowles
Are their males subjects, and at their controules:
Man more divine, the Master of all these,
Lord of the wide world, and wilde watry seas,
Indued with intellectuall sense and soules,
Of more preheminence then <u>fish</u> and fowles,
Are masters to their females, and their Lords   (F *CE* 2.1.18–24)

1.3.2 PRONOUNS

(Abbott, 205–43)

1.3.2.0 Overview

Pronouns are a set of **grammatical, function words**, used to replace fully lexical nouns. For example:

What's the Boy *Malcolme*?
Was <u>he</u> not borne of woman?   (F *Mac* 5.3.3–4)

where 'he' replaces 'the Boy *Malcolme*'. Pronouns have a **referent** (a thing to which they refer), and they agree with it in terms of gender and number (here, 'he' is masculine and singular). In this case, the referent of 'he' is explicitly present in the text before the pronoun occurs, and is termed the **antecedent** (literally: 'going before').

Although they have very similar functions, pronouns can be distinguished from full nouns in various ways. Most pronouns, for example, when they function as the head of a noun phrase, cannot appear with any other elements (such as determiners or any kind of pre- or post-head modification):

(I)	wrote	(a historical novel)
*(The I)	wrote	(a historical novel)

Possessive pronouns are exceptions to this, since they typically appear as pre-head modification:

(I)	wrote	(my historical novel)

(and see 1.3.2j for rare examples of pronouns taking modification).

As well as this failure to allow modification, pronouns behave differently from other nouns in two significant ways:

1 They mark shifts from singular to plural by changes in form rather than the addition of -s (for example: I → we, he → they).

2 They mark shifts in grammatical function by changes in form; thus

subject		*object*
(I)	asked	(her)
nominative		*accusative*

becomes, when the functions are reversed:

subject		*object*
(She)	asked	(me)
nominative		*accusative*

(Contrast this with 'Suzanne phoned Jonathan' versus 'Jonathan phoned Suzanne' where there is no shift in form on the full nouns.)

The marking of case (for example **nominative** and **accusative**) is an area of long-term change and high variability in English. Old English supported four main cases:

nominative	used to mark **subjects**
accusative	used to mark **objects**
dative	used to mark **indirect objects**, motion, and for various other relationships
genitive	used to mark possession

Pronouns, nouns, determiners and adjectives all changed their form to mark their grammatical role, much as words in Modern German do today. Languages which mark grammatical role in this way – usually by adding inflectional endings to the end of words – are termed **synthetic**.

However, even in the Old English period the synthetic marking of case was breaking down: differences between inflectional endings became blurred, and the inflections were typically **levelled** and then lost. Nouns, adjectives and determiners had lost all inflectional case marking by the Middle English period. As English lost inflectional case marking, grammatical information which had been carried synthetically by inflections shifted to being marked by word order (with clauses tending towards *subject–verb–object* order). Many of the functions of **dative** and genitive case marking were taken over by prepositional constructions (indirect objects and motion were marked by *to* constructions, for example). English thus shifted from being a synthetic language to being an **analytic** one.

Only the pronouns retained any kind of consistent case marking, probably because their shifts in form involved the whole word rather than simple inflectional endings. Pronoun case distinctions were thus more robust phonetically than inflectional endings.

However, the pronoun system did not resist change completely: English shifted from being a language which distinguished four or more cases to one distinguishing three or fewer: *subject, possessive, non-subject*.

A long-term tendency in English was for the **non-subject** cases, dative and accusative, to fall together, so that only one form was used for both, and for the resulting form to spread into all non-subject roles (and some where the subject role was ambiguous or unclear). In spoken and non-standard English there seems to be a tendency for non-subject forms to generalize, replacing even subject forms. Thus:

you	replaces	ye
me	replaces	I
thee	replaces	thou

This tendency, however, has been slowed and disrupted by prescriptivism.

Because of this history of change, Early Modern English shows considerable variation in the pronoun forms chosen for certain slots. It is important to remember, however, that it is inaccurate to ascribe this variation to ignorance or neglect (as Abbott tends to), either on Shakespeare's part or on that of his characters. The variation does not carry the stylistic dimensions it might if found in a Present-day English text.

Since Abbott devotes so much space to anomalous pronouns, I

cover the topic twice: once in the sections devoted to the respective pronouns, and once in a general section on anomalous pronouns (1.3.2g).

1.3.2a First person singular pronouns

Type: I   me   mine/my
(Abbott, 209, 210, 237)

The following table shows the development of the first person singular pronouns in English from the Old English to the Early Modern period.

	Old English	Middle English	Early Modern English
Nominative	ic	ich/I	I
Accusative	me	me	me
Dative	me	me	——
Genitive	min	min/mi	mine/my

I

The nominative form of the first person singular pronoun *I* can be seen from this table to derive from a form which contained a **velar stop** (*ic*: [ɪk]) or **palatal fricative** (*ich*: [ɪtʃ]). Some southern rural dialects apparently still retained traces of this in the Early Modern period, if we accept Edgar's put-on peasant-speak in *King Lear* as in any way accurate:

> Chill not let go Zir,
> Without vurther 'casion   (F *KL* 4.6.232)

where 'Chill' is 'I will'.

Despite being the nominative form, *I* can occur in contexts where we would expect the accusative form (*me*):

> O time, thou must untangle this, not I   (F *TN* 2.2.39)

> *Du.*   Her husband, sirrah?
> *Vio.*   No my Lord, not I   (F *TN* 5.1.143)

> We are alone, here's none but thee, & I   (F *2H6* 1.2.69)

> all debts are cleerd between you and I   (Fp *MV* 3.2.317)

> You know my Father hath no childe, but I   (Fp *AYL* 1.2.16)

> Unlesse you would devise some vertuous lye,
> To doe more for me then mine owne desert,
> and hang more praise upon deceased I   (Q *Son* 72.5–6)

> which may make this Island
> Thine owne for ever, and I̱ thy *Caliban*
> for aye thy foot-licker (F *Tem* 4.1.216–18)

As with most anomalous forms, Abbott (205) takes a prescriptive view, labelling these instances of neglect or misuse of grammar. However, as was noted in the Overview, it can be argued that case distinctions (such as that between accusative and nominative) have broken down in English – and certainly if this were happening we would expect long-term variation between forms in all contexts.

Abbott suggests that euphony may be an element in pronoun choice. The first example above avoids the pairing 'thee and me', and others tend to occur after a dental consonant (while the example from the *Sonnets* is for rhyme). Euphony may be a conditioning factor, but given the variation inherent in the language (and continuing today) we do not need to look any further for an explanation. The most important thing to note is that these are not examples of hypercorrection, nor is Shakespeare putting 'incorrect' forms in the mouths of his characters for stylistic purposes.

Me

Abbott (210) cites the following as examples of *me* used for *I*. However, the fact that the pronouns are clearly in non-subject roles accounts for the use of the accusative form. Most present-day speakers of British English would find 'I' pedantic or downright ungrammatical in these contexts

> A man no mightier then thy selfe, or <u>me</u> (F *JC* 1.3.76)

> Is she as tall as <u>me</u>? (F *AC* 3.3.11)

Mine/my

Abbott (237) notes that either of these forms can occur before a vowel (or *h*), suggesting that *my* carries emphasis. For example:

> by <u>my</u> honour
> Depart untouch'd (F *JC* 3.1.141–2)

which contrasts nicely with the same character's

> Beleeve me for
> <u>mine</u> Honour, and have respect to <u>mine</u> Honor (Fp *JC* 3.2.13)

Similarly, in *2 Henry IV* Northumberland has 'my' in formal verse, while Falstaff has 'mine' in clearly informal prose:

> Alas (sweet Wife) <u>my</u> Honor is at pawne,
> And but my going, nothing can redeeme it   (F *2H4* 2.3.7–8)

> No abuse (Hall) on <u>mine</u> Honor, no abuse   (Fp *2H4* 2.4.310)

Choice of form is also likely to be affected by scansion and euphony.

1.3.2b Second person singular pronouns

Type: thou   thee   thy/thine
         you/ye   your
(Abbott, 212, 213, 221, 231--5, 236, 237, 241)

The following table shows the development of the second person singular pronouns in English from the Old English period to the Early Modern period

	Old English	Middle English	Early Modern English
Nominative	þu	þu/ye	thou/you/ye
Accusative	þe	þe/yow	thee/you/ye
Dative	þe	þe	——
Genitive	þin	þin/þi	thine/thy/your

Simply comparing the number of alternates in each column shows that the second person singular pronoun system becomes progressively more complex over time, with the greatest complexity in the Early Modern period. In the following section, I will first discuss the historical development of each form from the Old English to the Early Modern period, then look at the systems governing choice of the forms in use in the Early Modern period.

Thou

Thou derives from the Old English nominative singular form, *þu* (the letter form *þ* represents a **dental fricative** [ð] or [θ], as does the modern pair *th*). It is always restricted to the singular, and is usually found in nominative contexts (but see below for some rare exceptions).

Thee

Thee derives from the Old English dative/accusative singular form, *þe* (with *þ* again representing a dental fricative). Like *thou*, it is always restricted to the singular, and it is usually found in accusative contexts (but see below for exceptions).

Ye

Ye derives from the Old English *plural* nominative form. After being borrowed into the singular paradigm in the Middle English period, it also shifts case, and is used in both nominative and accusative contexts (see *ye/you* below).

You

You derives from the Old English *plural* accusative form. Like *ye*, after crossing the number boundary during the Middle English period, it also crosses the case division, and appears in both accusative and nominative contexts.

Thou/you, thee/you, thy/your

In Old English, the two forms of the second person pronoun were rigidly separated by number: *þ*-forms (later *th*-forms) were strictly singular; *g*-forms (later *y*-forms) strictly plural. In the Middle English period, however, plural *y*-forms began to appear in singular contexts when the person addressed was powerful (a monarch or bishop, for example). This 'respectful' usage was probably modelled on similar usages in Latin and French.

By the Early Modern period, a complex system of choice between *th*-forms and *y*-forms in the singular had developed. Such systems are common in the languages of the world: borrowing plural pronouns into the singular as a marker of respect seems to be a 'natural' change. French, German, Spanish and Finnish are amongst the European languages which show such behaviour.

The basic factor determining choice of *th*- or *y*- pronoun in Early Modern English is social relationship: *th*-forms are used *down* the social hierarchy; *y*-forms *up* it. This means that those in authority – kings, lords, husbands, fathers, masters – can use *th*-forms to those in subordinate roles: subjects, vassals, wives, children, servants. Subordinates use *y*-forms in return. Social equals usually exchange mutual *y*-forms in the Early Modern period.

Examples of social distance being marked in this way are fairly easy to find:

> *Yorke.* Base Dunghill Villaine, and Mechanicall,
> Ile have <u>thy</u> Head for this <u>thy</u> Traytors speech:
> I doe beseech <u>your</u> Royal Majestie,
> Let him have all the rigor of the Law   (F *2H6* 1.3.193–6)

In the first two lines of this speech, the nobleman York addresses an armourer, who is, as York is at pains to point out, 'Mechanicall' (a manual labourer); in the second, he addresses the King.

In *Julius Caesar*, Brutus distinguishes the rank of his friends (*y*-forms) from that of his servant, Strato:

> Farewell to <u>you</u>, and <u>you</u>, and <u>you</u> *Volumnius*,
> *Strato* <u>thou</u> hast bin all this while asleepe:
> Farewell to <u>thee</u>, to *Strato*   (F *JC* 5.5.31–3)

Similarly, in *King Lear*, Gloucester marks an assumed social difference when he addresses the disguised Edgar:

> *Edg.* Now fare <u>ye</u> well, good Sir   (F *KL* 4.6.32)

> *Glo.* Now Fellow, fare <u>thee</u> well   (F *KL* 4.6.41)

The social semantic for pronoun choice was a powerful force. At the end of *2 Henry IV*, Falstaff badly misjudges his relationship to the newly crowned Henry V:

> *The Trumpets sound. Enter King Henrie the*
> *Fift, Brothers, Lord Chiefe*
> *Justice.*

> *Falst.* Save <u>thy</u> Grace, King Hall, my Royal Hall.
> *Pist.* The heavens <u>thee</u> guard, and keepe, most royall
> Impe of fame.
> *Fal.* 'Save <u>thee</u> my sweet Boy.
> *King.* My Lord Chiefe Justice, speake to that vaine   5
> man.
> *Ch.Just.* Have <u>you your</u> wits?
> Know <u>you</u> what 'tis <u>you</u> speake?
> *Falst.* My King, my Jove; I speake to <u>thee</u>, my heart.

> (F *2H4* 5.5.41–6)

Falstaff's choice of *th*-forms for this formal, public occasion, and to address his King, is crazily inappropriate (formal terms of address like 'Grace' and 'King' rarely, if ever, collocate with *th*-forms). Henry's response is instructive: he refuses even to address Falstaff directly ('My Lord Chiefe Justice, speake to that vaine man'); but the Lord Chief Justice's response is even more interesting. He does not accuse Falstaff of being rude: he assumes he must be mad – 'Have you your wits? Know you what 'tis you speake?' The social semantic is so powerful that the Lord Chief Justice believes that only a lunatic would transgress it.

Apparent departures from this social semantic can be deceptive. In *Richard III*, Clarence first addresses his lower-class murderers with *th*-forms, as the model would predict, but then apparently shifts into *y*-forms (the individual murderers are given numbers as speech prefixes in the following; when they speak together, the prefix is '*Am.*' for 'all murderers'):

> *Cla.*   Where art thou keeper, give me a cup of wine.
> 1   <u>You</u> shall have wine enough my Lo: anon.
> *Cla.*   In Gods name what art <u>thou</u>.
> 2   A man as <u>you</u> are.
> *Cla.*   But not as I am, royall.   5
> 2   Nor <u>you</u> as we are, loyall.
> *Cla.*   <u>Thy</u> voice is thunder, but <u>thy</u> lookes are humble.
> 2   My voice is now the Kings, my lookes mine owne.
> *Cla.*   How darkly and how deadly doest <u>thou</u> speak:
> Tell me who are <u>you</u>, wherefore come <u>you</u> hither?   10
> *Am.*   To, to, to.
> *Cla.*   To murther me.   *Am.* I   (Q *R3* 1.4.153–63)

In fact there is a *number* change here: Clarence shifts from addressing one murderer to addressing them both (as their joint answer shows). The grammar of the passage thus confirms the decision of most editors to follow the Quarto speech prefixes rather than the Folio ones here, since the Folio assigns 'To, to, to' and 'I' to the first murderer alone.

Some shifts in pronoun use, however, cannot be explained by a shift in number. Because of the respect encoded in the use of *y*-forms, it was possible to insult someone by using an unexpected *th*-form:

> *Warw.*   Whether <u>your</u> Grace be worthy, yea or no,
> Dispute not that, *Yorke* is the worthyer.
> *Card.*   Ambitious *Warwicke*, let <u>thy</u> betters speake.
> *Warw.*   The Cardinall's not my better in the field.
> *Buck.*   All in this presence are <u>thy</u> betters, *Warwicke*
> (F *2H6* 1.3.107–11)

These are all noble characters, so the Cardinal and Buckingham's *th*-forms to Warwick are a calculated social put-down.

It's a short step from this kind of playing with the social semantics of *th*- and *y*-forms to the development, as happens in English, of a second principle governing choice of the forms: emotion.

Choice of, and movement between, the forms can encode anger or affection. In the opening scene of *Julius Caesar*, the tribunes Marullus and Flavius address a crowd of 'mechanicals'. First castigating a carpenter for not wearing the signs of his profession, using *th*-forms in the process, Marullus then shifts pronoun, apparently being conciliatory, to the next man:

> *Mar.* Where is <u>thy</u> Leather Apron, and <u>thy</u> Rule?
> What dost <u>thou</u> with <u>thy</u> best Apparrell on?
> <u>You</u> Sir, what Trade are <u>you</u>?
> *Cobl.* Truely Sir, in respect of a fine Workman, I am
> but, as <u>you</u> would say, a Cobler.
> *Mar.* But what Trade art *thou*? Answer me directly. (Fp *JC* 1.1.7–12)

When he thinks he is being quibbled-with ('cobbler' could mean 'a botcher' in a general sense, as well as a fixer of shoes), Marullus switches back to *th*-forms in irritation.

Confusingly, anger is not always marked by a switch from *y*-forms into *th*-forms. Depending on the context, it can be marked by the reverse movement. Masters normally address their servants with *th*-forms, so a shift into *y*-forms can mark an increased distance in the relationship. For example, in *The Comedy of Errors*, Antipholus and Dromio of Syracuse begin with the predicted exchange of non-reciprocal pronouns: Antipholus calls Dromio 'thou', and his servant Dromio replies with *y*-forms:

> *Ant.* Goe beare it to the Centaure, where we host,
> And stay there *Dromio*, till I come to thee;
> Within this houre it will be dinner time,
> Till that Ile view the manners of the towne,
> Peruse the traders, gaze upon the buildings,   5
> And then returne and sleepe within mine Inne,
> For with long travailel I am stiffe and wearie.
> Get <u>thee</u> away.
> *Dro.* Many a man would take <u>you</u> at <u>your</u> word,
> And goe indeede, having so good a meane   (F *CE* 1.2.9–18)

Despite the non-reciprocal pronouns, the relationship between the two is close, as Antipholus says of Dromio after he has left:

A trustie villaine sir, that very oft,
When I am dull with care and melancholly,
Lightens my humour with his merry jests   (F CE 1.2.19–21)

When Dromio of Ephesus enters a few lines later, Antipholus takes him for his servant, and employs *th*-forms:

Here comes the almanacke of my true date:
What now? How chance <u>thou</u> art return'd so soone   (F CE 1.2.41–2)

Irritated by Dromio's (to him) unintelligible answer about being late for dinner, Antipholus shifts from affectionate *th*-forms into distant *y*-forms (note also the distancing 'sir'):

Stop in <u>your</u> winde sir, tell me this I pray?
Where have <u>you</u> left the money that I gave <u>you</u>?   (F CE 1.2.53–4)

Similar reversals of the connotations of the forms can occur within lovers' discourse: conventionally carried out in *th*-forms, but often switching to *y*-forms, perhaps because the very conventionality of *th*-forms can make them seem insincere (usage in the *Sonnets* seems to follow this pattern in a subtle and sophisticated way).

In trying to read the significance of second person pronoun forms in Early Modern English we therefore have to be aware of the presence of two systems governing choice:

1   a relatively fixed social semantic

2   an unfixed emotional or affective semantic

We also need to be aware that these two systems interact, and that we can state general tendencies and expectations based on semantic 1, but that these are always reversible when semantic 2 comes into play. Choice of form has to be read in terms of both broad social context and the immediate context of the discourse.

It is also important to remember that *th-/y*-form usage as represented in Shakespeare's plays is unlikely to mirror actual usage in the Early Modern period. Shakespeare can be shown to differ in his use of the pronoun forms from other Early Modern playwrights (he is far more open to the use of *th*-forms generally, and to switching forms between the same characters). It seems likely that Early Modern drama generally, and Shakespeare especially, over-represent the frequency of *th*-forms: evidence from court records suggests that *th*-forms were highly **marked** quite early in the sixteenth century.

The marked status of *th*-forms is underlined by their appearance in certain well-defined contexts, where their use is almost mandatory:

absence, archaism, apostrophe, and address to animals and spirits. This behaviour – increasing restriction to a group of fixed, specialized contexts – is characteristic of variants which are being lost from a language.

Absence/aside

Th-forms are usual when the person addressed is either offstage, or is not meant to hear what is said. In *Julius Caesar* 1.2, Brutus and Cassius initially exchange the *y*-forms the social semantic would predict for two upper-class Romans, but Cassius shifts when Brutus exits:

> *Cassi.* No, *Cæsar* hath it not: but <u>you</u>, and I,
> And honest *Caska*, we have the Falling sicknesse.
> . . .
>
> *Brut.* For this time I will leave you:
> To morrow, if you please to speake with me,
> I will come home to you: or if you will,
> Come home to me, and I will wait for you.
>   *Cassi.* I will doe so: till then, thinke of the World.
>   *Exit Brutus.*
> Well *Brutus*, <u>thou</u> art Noble   (F *JC* 1.2.252–3, 300–5)

Apostrophe

Possibly related to the use of *th*-forms for addressing absent speakers, *th*-forms are usual in apostrophe to gods and abstract personifications. Hence:

> Oh <u>thou</u> cleare god, and patron of all light   (Q *VA* 860)

> Frailty, <u>thy</u> name is woman   (F *Ham* 1.2.146)

>   O Murd'rous slumbler!
> Layest <u>thou</u> thy Leaden Mace upon my Boy,
> That playes <u>thee</u> Musicke?   (F *JC* 4.3.266–8)

Animals

As with God, so with animals: *th*-forms are generally expected towards animals, and Launce follows this in his address to his dog Crab, except for one *y*-form, which looks like an attempt to avoid the phonetically clumsy 'thou servedest':

thou

think'st not of this now: nay, I remember the tricke <u>you</u>
serv'd me, when I tooke my leave of Madam *Silvia*: did
not I bid <u>thee</u> still marke me, and doe as I doe, when did'st
<u>thou</u> see me heave up my leg, and make water against a
Gentlewomans farthingale? did'st <u>thou</u> ever see me doe
such a trick?   (Fp *TGV* 4.4.33–9)

Ghosts and spirits

Again, the expectation here is for *th*-forms, and this is confirmed by
Brutus' conversation with Caesar's ghost:

Enter the Ghost of Cæsar.

How ill this Taper burnes. Ha! Who comes heere?
I thinke it is the weakenesse of mine eyes
That shapes this monstrous Apparition.
It comes upon me: Art <u>thou</u> any thing?
Art <u>thou</u> some God, some Angell, or some Divell,   5
That mak'st my blood cold, and my haire to stare?
Speake to me, what <u>thou</u> art.
    Ghost. <u>Thy</u> evill Spirit *Brutus*.
    Bru. Why com'st <u>thou</u>?
    Ghost. To tell <u>thee thou</u> shalt see me at *Philippi*.   10
    Brut. Well: then I shall see <u>thee</u> againe?
    Ghost. I, at *Philippi*.
    Brut. Why I will see <u>thee</u> at *Philippi* then:
Now I have taken heart, <u>thou</u> vanishest.
Ill Spirit, I would hold more talke with <u>thee</u>   (F *JC* 4.3.274–87)

As with other apparently fixed conventions of pronoun use, however,
this expectation can be varied according to the affective semantic. On
its first appearance, Hamlet consistently addresses the ghost of his
father with *th*-forms, stressing his doubts about its origins:

Enter Ghost.

  Hor. Looke my Lord, it comes.
  Ham. Angels and Ministers of Grace defend us:
Be <u>thou</u> a Spirit of health or Goblin damn'd,
Bring with <u>thee</u> ayres from Heaven, or blasts from Hell,
Be <u>thy</u> events wicked or charitable,
<u>Thou</u> com'st in such a questionable shape

That I will speake to <u>thee</u>. Ile call <u>thee</u> Hamlet,
King, Father, Royall Dane   (F *Ham* 1.4.38–45)

On the ghost's second appearance, however, when he has killed Polonius, and is apparently determined to revenge his father, Hamlet uses *y*-forms, explicitly acknowledging that the ghost is his father:

> *Enter Ghost.*
>
> *Ham.*   A King of shreds and patches.
> Save me: and hover o're me with your wings
> You heavenly Guards. What would <u>you</u> gracious figure?
>   *Qu.*   Alas he's mad.
>   *Ham.*   Do <u>you</u> not come <u>your</u> tardy Sonne to chide,
> That, laps'd in Time and Passion, lets go by
> Th'important acting of <u>your</u> dread command?   (F *Ham* 3.4.103–9)

Archaism

Th-forms are the **recessive** set in the *y-*/*th*- pairing: in other words, they are the set which will disappear from the standard language. In keeping with other instances of competition between older and newer sets of forms, the *th*-forms quickly become associated with archaic or formal language, and are used in contexts favouring linguistic conservatism. Hence the apparently anomalous convention of using *th*-forms to God – who might reasonably be expected to receive *y*-forms out of respect!

Hence also the 'chivalric' use of *th*-foms, frequent in the history plays, when formal challenges and defiance are issued. These do not necessarily imply contempt, as the exchanges between Henry and the French herald Mountjoy show in *Henry V*:

> Once more I come to know of <u>thee</u> King *Harry*,
> If for <u>thy</u> Ransome <u>thou</u> wilt now compound,
> Before <u>thy</u> most assured Overthrow:
> For certainly, <u>thou</u> art so neere the Gulfe,
> <u>Thou</u> needs must be englutted   (F *HS* 4.3.79–83)

But of course contempt and anger are often not far away from a formal challenge, as is shown by Sir Toby's celebrated advice to Andrew Aguecheek when he writes to challenge the disguised Viola:

> Go, write it in a martial hand, be curst and briefe:
> it is no matter how wittie, so it bee eloquent and full of
> invention: taunt him with the license of Inke: if thou
> <u>thou'st</u> him some thrice, it shall not be amisse   (Fp *TN* 3.2.40–4)

Using *th*-forms ('thouing') to address the supposed 'him' fits both a 'martial' style and the desire to insult. Toby's use of the familiar *thou* to Aguecheek immediately before his advice to use it to challenge Viola neatly illustrates the polysemy of *th*-forms at this time.

The archaic-religious and archaic-legal connotation of *th*-forms are illustrated in *Richard III* when Clarence tries to plead for his life to his murderers. Addressing the two of them as *you*, he then slips into a biblical *thou* when quoting a commandment; unfortunately for him, the murderers pick up on this, and shift their usage, up till now respectful *y*-forms, to the *th*-forms of chivalric and legal accusation:

> *Clar.* Erroneous Vassals, the great King of Kings
> Hath in the Table of his Law commanded
> That <u>thou</u> shalt do no murther. Will you then
> Spurne at his Edict, and fulfill a Mans?
> Take heed: for he holds Vengeance in his hand,   5
> To hurle upon their heads that breake his Law.
>   2 And that same Vengeance doth he hurle on <u>thee</u>,
> For false Forswearing, and for murther too:
> <u>Thou</u> did'st receive the Sacrament, to fight
> In quarrell of the House of Lancaster.   10
>   1 And like a Traitor to the name of God,
> Did'st breake that Vow, and with <u>thy</u> treacherous blade,
> Unrip'st the Bowels of <u>thy</u> Sov'raignes Sonne.
>   2 Whom <u>thou</u> was't sworne to cherish and defend.
>   1 How canst <u>thou</u> urge Gods dreadfull Law to us,   15
> When <u>thou</u> hast broke it in such deere degree?   (F *R3* 1.4.184–99)

The extent to which *th*-forms are archaic and literary by the early years of the seventeenth century may be shown by the highly unusual pattern of second person pronoun use in Shakespeare and Fletcher's *Henry VIII*. This play shows an almost complete avoidance of *th*-forms, something unusual for both playwrights in their work elsewhere. It may be, given the play's stress on truth and accurate representation of court life, that the playwrights consciously or unconsciously avoided *th*-forms in a desire not to produce 'costume' history, more accurately representing actual usage of their own time.

Thee/thou

As stated in the Overview, it can be argued that the case system of Old English is simplified successively in Middle, Early Modern and Present-day English into a binary subject/non-subject system where speakers use the non-subject form as a default, except in cases where the context makes the pronoun unambiguously subject. This explains the tendency for accusative forms to spread generally, and especially for their appearance in post-verbal contexts where their position makes them look non-subject like, whatever a strict application of grammatical rules might imply. Abbott's prescriptivist tendencies thus lead him to worry unduly about **imperative** instances such as:

Blossome, speed <u>thee</u> well	(F *WT* 3.3.46)
Good Margaret runne <u>thee</u> to the parlour	(F *MA* 3.1.1)
Stand <u>thee</u> by Frier	(F *MA* 4.1.22)
Hearke <u>thee</u>, a word	(F *Cym* 1.6.32)

Abbott also worries about contexts after *to be*, where prescriptive rules require nominative forms (for example 'It is <u>I</u>'), but usage almost always supplies accusative, or non-subject forms (for example 'It is <u>me</u>'):

I would not be <u>thee</u> Nunckle	(Fp *KL* 1.4.182–3)
Ape. Art thou proud yet?	
Tim. I, that I am not <u>thee</u>	(F *Tim* 4.3.277–8)
it is <u>thee</u> I fear	(F *2H6* 4.1.117)

Generic *your*

Generic *your* is used to express a general truth about something in an informal, colloquial way, hence Hamlet's

<blockquote>
<u>Your</u> worm
is <u>your</u> onely Emperor for diet. We fat all creatures else
to fat us, and we fat our selfe for Magots. <u>Your</u> fat King,
and <u>your</u> leane Begger is but variable service to dishes,
but to one Table that's the end   (Fp *Ham* 4.3.21–5)
</blockquote>

There is no real sense of possession here – the *your* implies that the thing named shares some generic feature of the category to which it belongs, and which is well known. Similar usages are found in spoken British English today. Even when used in contexts where the possession sense is possible, such as Lepidus lecturing the Egyptian Romans about their own adopted country, it is the generalized truth sense which comes through most clearly:

<blockquote>
<u>Your</u> Serpent of Egypt, is bred now of <u>your</u> mud
by the operation of <u>your</u> Sun: so is <u>your</u> Crocodile. (Fp *AC* 2.7.26–7)
</blockquote>

As with 'dative' pronouns (1.3.2i), the construction is informal – note that all of the examples given here come from prose contexts – and the possessive pronoun is used to imply easy familiarity. Hence there is some variation between the possessive pronouns in this context:

> But if you mouth it,
>
> as many of <u>your</u> Players do (Fp *Ham* 3.2.2–3)
>
> but if you mouth it as many of <u>our</u> Players do (Q2p *Ham* 3.2.2–3)

Ye/you

As noted above, Old English made a strict case distinction between *ye* and *you*, with *ye* nominative (subject) and *you* accusative (object). In general use, this distinction had completely broken down by the Early Modern period, and the two forms seem to be interchangeable. The 1611 Authorized Version of the Bible misrepresents 'real' seventeenth-century English, since the translators followed Tyndale (1534) in distinguishing the forms; for example:

> Ask and it shall be given <u>you</u>. Seek and <u>ye</u> shall find
>> (Tyndale: Matthew, 7)
>
> Ask, and it shall be given <u>you</u>; seek, and <u>ye</u> shall find
>> (Authorized Version: Matthew, 7.7)

Th-forms deleted

Th-forms can be deleted where the verb is inflected with the second person singular inflection. Hence:

> Didst thou
>
> not see her paddle with the palme of his hand? Didst ^ not marke that? (Fp *Oth* 2.1.251–2)
>
> Wilt ^ dine with me *Apemantus*? (F *Tim* 1.1.203)
>
> Noblest of men, woo't ^ dye?
>
> Hast thou no care of me (F *AC* 4.15.59–60)

1.3.2c Third person singular pronouns

Type: he she it hit
(Abbott, 211, 218, 226, 227, 228, 229)

Masculine third person singular pronouns

Type: he   a   him   his

The following table shows the development of the masculine third person singular pronouns in English:

	Old English	Middle English	Early Modern English
Nominative	he	he/a	he/a
Accusative	hine	hine/him	him
Dative	him	him	——
Genitive	his	his	his

He

He, the nominative form, is normally associated with subject roles, but it can crop up in non-subject roles:

'Tis better thee without, then <u>he</u> within   (F *Mac* 3.4.14)

Here, it is perhaps chosen for the sake of euphony with 'thee'. It also occurs in syntactically ambiguous contexts:

Which, of <u>he</u>, or Adrian, for a good wager,
First begins to crow?   (F *Tem* 2.1.28–9)

Here 'he' is the object of the preposition 'of', which might prompt accusative case (*him*), but 'he' is also the subject of 'begins', and occupies clause-initial position – so nominative marking appears. Similarly:

And yet no man like <u>he</u>, doth grieve my heart   (F *RJ* 3.5.83)

where 'like' might be expected to prompt accusative case ('like him'), but 'he' is also the subject of 'doth grieve', and appears before the verb in the clause.

In some contexts where *he* is not clause-initial, it may be selected as more emphatic than *him*:

And were I any thing but what I am,
I would wish me onely <u>he</u>   (F *Cor* 1.1.230–1)

(Though euphony is possibly at work here as well.)

The effect of the pronoun being clause-initial is strong:

Thus <u>he</u> that over-ruld, I over-swayed   (Q *VA* 109)

which could be paraphrased as 'I over-swayed <u>him</u>'. Similarly:

And <u>he</u>, my husband best of all affects   (F *MW* 4.4.86)

That is, 'my husband likes <u>him</u> best'.

He plus first person

There is one curious instance of *he* taking first person verb agreement in Shakespeare, which comes when Petruchio declares

> For I am he <u>am</u> borne to tame you *Kate*   (F *TS* 2.1.269)

The relevant structure here is the relative clause after 'he': 'for I am he <u>who is</u> born to tame you'. Relative clauses frequently trigger unexpected agreement on the verb in the relative clause (see section 1.4.2), but this is almost always an unexpected third person singular agreement – what we ought to have here, but do not get. This could be an anticipatory setting error by the compositor, but the verb form may be the product of the tendency for Early Modern pronouns to shift word class (see *she/her* below) – with 'he' not being analysed as a pronoun here, and so not triggering third person agreement on 'am'.

A

The use of *a* for unstressed *he* is common in Middle English, especially in the south and west. Shakespeare's linguistic roots in this dialect area make him one of the final citations for the usage in the *OED*. As well as lack of stress, the form implies informality, but it is highly unstable textually, and liable to be changed to *he* by scribes or compositors:

> Now might I doe it, but now <u>a</u> is a praying,
> And now Ile doo't, and so <u>a</u> goes to heaven . . .
> <u>A</u> tooke my father grosly full of bread   (Q2p *Ham* 1.3.73–4, 80)

All of these instances of *a* in Q2 appear as *he* in F. Similarly:

> He
> is but a Knight, is <u>a</u>?   (Fp *2H6* 4.2.108)

appears in the Quarto as:

> hees but a knight is <u>he</u>   (Qp *2H6* 4.2.108)

Him

In the following instances, the pronouns are the subjects of distant **main verbs**, but carry the object form because of a closer verb in a relative clause:

> <u>Him</u> I accuse:
> The City Ports by this hath enter'd   (F *Cor* 5.6.5)

'Him' is the subject of 'hath enter'd' (a rewording would be 'he hath enter'd . . .'), but the pronoun appears in accusative form because the person in question is the object of the relative clause: 'Him [that] I accuse . . .'. The principle of proximity wins out. Similarly:

I, better then <u>him</u> I am before knowes mee   (Fp *AYL* 1.1.43)

where the main clause is 'he knows me', but the proximity of the relative, 'I am before (him)', triggers the accusative case on 'him'. Also:

Better to leave undone, then by our deed
Acquire too high a Fame, when <u>him</u> we serve's away   (F *AC* 3.1.14–15)

Feminine third person singular pronouns

Type: she   her   hers

The development of the feminine third person singular pronouns in English is as follows:

	Old English	**Middle English**	**Early Modern English**
Nominative	heo/hio	ho/he/hi/scæ/scho	she
Accusative	hie/hi	hi/heo/hire	her
Dative	hire	?hire	——
Genitive	hire	hire/hore	her/hers

She/her

As I have suggested in regard to the other pronouns, there seems to be a general tendency in English for accusative forms to move into all non-subject slots. The feminine singular pronoun behaves slightly differently, however. As can be seen from the table, there has been considerable change in the form of this pronoun, especially in the nominative – and linguists are still not agreed on the history of *she*. Whatever its history, this form behaves differently to other nominative pronouns (such as *he*). Abbott notes that it is much more likely than *he* to be used as a noun in the sense of 'woman':

And yet by heaven I thinke my love as rare,
As any <u>she</u> beli'd with false compare   (Q *Son* 130.13–14)

And *she* often crops up in accusative contexts, indicating that *she*, rather than *her*, may be the default form for speakers:

Yes, you have seene *Cassio* and <u>she</u> together   (F *Oth* 4.2.3)

So sawcy with the hand of <u>she</u> heere, what's her name   (F *AC* 3.13.98)

Apparent position can be as important in assigning case as actual grammatical context. In the following, which Abbott found a 'remarkable anomaly' (211), *she* is selected, rather than *her*, because *she* looks like a subject, coming at the start of a relative clause:

> Praise him that got thee, <u>she</u> that gave thee sucke (F *TC* 2.3.241)

The phonological similarity between *thee* and *she* may also be relevant here.

Neuter third person singular pronouns

Type: it   his   its

The development of the third person neuter singular pronoun in English is as follows:

	Old English	**Middle English**	**Early Modern English**
Nominative	hit	hit	it
Accusative	hit	hit	it
Dative	him	?him/hit	———
Genitive	his	his/hit	his/its/it

Genitive forms

The unmarked form of the neuter genitive in Shakespeare is *his*:

> His Coward lippes did from their colour flye,
> And that same Eye, whose bend doth awe the World,
> Did lose <u>his</u> Lustre (F *JC* 1.2.121–3)

> In such a time as this, it is not meet
> That every nice offence should beare <u>his</u> Comment. (F *JC* 4.3.7–8)

Its can be found occasionally in Shakespeare:

> Heaven grant us <u>its</u> peace, but not the King
> of *Hungaries* (Fp *MM* 1.2.4)

where the marked form is probably prompted by the contrastive emphasis: *Heaven's* peace rather than the King's. Instances of *its* are very unevenly distributed in the first Folio, however, with five out of a total of ten in one play: *The Winter's Tale* (1.2.151, 152, 157, 266; 3.3.46). This strongly suggests that they have been introduced by a compositor or scribe.

The older, uninflected genitive *it* is slightly more frequent than *its* in the Folio (it occurs fourteen times):

The innocent milke in <u>it</u> most innocent mouth.   (F *WT* 3.2.100)

Both Quarto and first Folio versions of *King Lear* have *it* in the following:

>   the Hedge-Sparrow
> fed the Cuckoo so long, that it's had <u>it</u> head bit off by <u>it</u>
> young   (Fp *KL* 1.4.213–14)

which is evidence for a certain amount of textual stability in the form, but the speed with which the form is being lost from the language is shown by the replacement of all of these *it* forms with *its* by the Third Folio. The context of many uninflected *it* forms suggests that it has an archaic but informal connotation, being associated with proverbs and folk-wisdom.

Indefinite *it*

> Type: She sweeps <u>it</u> through the court with troops of ladies
> (Abbott, 226)

As today, *it* can be used with no specific antecedent or referent, either in subject position ('<u>It</u> is raining'), or, more frequently, in object position:

> Not all these Lords do vex me halfe so much,
> As that prowd Dame, the Lord Protectors Wife:
> She sweeps <u>it</u> through the Court with troups of Ladies
>
>   (F *2H6* 1.3.75–7)

The use of *it* in this way is very common where noun–verb conversion has taken place because the presence of a dummy object emphasizes the functional shift:

> Foote <u>it</u> featly heere, and there   (F *Tem* 1.2.381)

>   a threepence bow'd would hire me
> Old as I am, to Queene <u>it</u>   (F *H8* 2.3.36–7)

> Lord *Angelo* Dukes <u>it</u> well in his absence   (Fp *MM* 3.2.91)

Emphatic *it*

> Type: There was <u>it</u> for which my sinews shall be stretched upon him
> (Abbott, 227)

As with *she* ('any she belied with false compare'), *it* can be used as a full noun in positions of stress or emphasis and before a relative clause where Present-day English would require an element such as 'the thing' or a demonstrative such as *that*:

> There was <u>it</u>
> For which my sinewes shall be stretcht upon him   (F *Cor* 5.6.44–5)

where modern usage would require: 'that was <u>the thing</u> for which my sinews will be stretched upon him'. Similarly:

> for that's <u>it</u>, that alwayes
> makes a good voyage of nothing   (Fp *TN* 2.4.78–9)

> <u>it</u> holds cur-
> rant that I told you yesternight   (Fp *1H4* 2.1.52–3)

See also section 1.4.2 on relative clauses.

`1.3.2d` First person plural pronouns

Type: we   us   our
(Abbott, 215)

The development of the first person plural pronouns in English is as follows:

	Old English	**Middle English**	**Early Modern English**
Nominative	we	we	we
Accusative	us	us	us
Dative	us	us	———
Genitive	ure	ure	our

Shall's

Elided *us* is found in apparently nominative contexts associated with the **modal verb** *shall*:

Say, where shall'<u>s</u> lay him?   (F *Cym* 4.2.233)

Shall'<u>s</u> have a play of this?   (F *Cym* 5.5.228)

shall'<u>s</u> attend you there?   (F *WT* 1.2.178)

The *OED* (*us* I 5a) sees this as dialectal – a substitution of one case form for another. Abbott suggests that it goes back to *shall* as an impersonal verb, with the sense of necessity or obligation. Hence a possible paraphrase for the first example would be 'Where is it necessary <u>for us</u> to lay him?'

1.3.2e Second person plural pronouns

Type: you   ye   your   yours

The development of the plural second person pronouns in English is as follows:

	Old English	Middle English	Early Modern English
Nominative	ge	ye	you/ye
Accusative	eow	ow/you	you/ye
Dative	eow	ow/you	——
Genitive	eower	ower/your	your/yours

As has been noted above, the plural second person pronoun paradigm eventually merges with the singular paradigm. Similar developments in form are found: *you*, originally accusative, gradually replaces *ye* as the nominative form.

The loss of number distinction in the second person pronoun in Standard English is an unusual development, since most languages retain such a distinction. Not surprisingly, many dialects of English have reinvented plural forms: *youse* in northern dialects of British English; *you-all* in southern American English dialects. In Standard English, speakers often find other ways of marking plurality with *you*, and in Shakespeare we find

<blockquote>
where, as <u>all you</u> know,
Harmlesse Richard was murthered traiterously   (F 2H6 2.2.25–6)
</blockquote>

The Arden 3 editor notes that the phrase is found in Shakespeare's source for this line, and also that it is used elsewhere in Shakespeare where more than one is addressed:

<blockquote>
Why then good-morrow to you all (my Lords:)
Have you read o're the Letters that I sent you?   (F 2H4 3.1.35–6)
</blockquote>

1.3.2f Third person plural pronouns

Type: they   them   their   theirs   ??her
(Abbott, 214)

The development of the plural third person pronouns in English is as follows:

	Old English	Middle English	Early Modern English
Nominative	hie/hi	hi/ho/heo/þay	they
Accusative	hie/hi	hi/hem/him	them

Dative	him	?hom/heom	——
Genitive	hira/hiera/heora/ hiora	hore/heore/þayr	their/theirs/??her

th- versus h-forms: *her* for *their*?

As will be seen from the table, the third person plural pronouns in English underwent a major change in form in the Middle English period, shifting from *h*-based forms to a set of forms beginning with a dental fricative (originally spelled with ð or þ, now *th*-based). The *th*-forms originated in the Scandinavian languages spoken in close proximity to northern English dialects in the Danelaw, and were presumably borrowed into English because the Old English *h*-forms were ambiguous with singular pronouns.

Although this change began in the north, it was complete, or virtually complete, in the south by the time of Shakespeare's birth, and there are no unambiguous instances of *h*-forms for plural third person pronouns in Shakespeare. Hence my question marks in the table above. There are, however, four instances where *her* appears in Folio or Quarto texts and editors have claimed that the form represents a third person plural genitive pronoun (that is, *their*):

> *Mess.* . . . Awake, awake, English Nobilitie,
> Let not slouth dimme your Honors, new begot;
> Cropt are the Flower-de-Luces in your Armes
> Of Englands Coat, one halfe is cut away.
>   *Exe.* Were our Teares wanting to this Funerall,
> These Tidings would call forth <u>her</u> flowing Tides. (F *1H6* 1.1.78–83)

There are three possible explanations for this form: (1) the compositor misread the copy and set *her* for *ther*; (2) the copy read *her* and it is a genuine *h*-form plural pronoun, representing one of the last such uses in English; (3) the antecedent of the pronoun is not 'Tidings' or 'Teares', but 'Englands', which is feminized and personified.

A second apparent plural *her* appears in *Othello*:

> And yet his trespasse, in our common reason,
> (Save that they say, the warres must make examples,
> Out of <u>her</u> best) is not almost a fault (Q *Oth* 3.3.65–7)

I have quoted from the First Quarto here, as that text has the clearest punctuation, but the Folio and all other Quartos also have *her* at this point. This agreement between otherwise quite divergent texts makes explanation 1, compositorial misreading of copy, unlikely, leaving 2, that it is a genuine plural *h*-form, and 3, that something about the antecedent triggers a singular *her,* as possible explanations.

I think that this is the best candidate for a genuine *h*-form plural in Shakespeare, but even here it is possible that the antecedent may have triggered a singular *her.* The noun *wars* behaves curiously in Shakespeare, sometimes being plural, sometimes singular, rather like an eel changing from a salt- to a fresh-water fish. Generally *wars* is marked as plural if a demonstrative is used: 'these wars', 'those wars'; but can trigger singular or plural agreement on any associated verb ('warres hath', F *AW* 1.1.191, but 'Warres point at me', F *Cym* 4.3.7). So it is possible that 'warres' is taken as a singular here, personified, and feminized (it may be significant that the only example I have been able to find of a singular demonstrative being used with *wars* occurs in *Othello*: 'This present Warres', F *Oth* 1.3.234).

The next candidate is found in the Folio text of *Troilus and Cressida*:

Take but Degree away, un-tune that string,
And hearke what Discord followes: . . .
Strength should be Lord of imbecility,
And the rude Sonne should strike his Father dead:
Force should be right, or rather, right and wrong,
(Betweene whose endlesse jarre, Justice resides)
Should loose her names, and so should Justice too

(F *TC* 1.3.109–10, 114–18)

The Folio's 'her' appears as 'their' in the Quarto, which suggests to me that this is an example of compositorial error: 'her' is one and a half lines from its referent ('right and wrong'), and it is sandwiched between two instances of 'Justice', which might very well trigger a singular feminine pronoun.

The final instance is found in *Titus Andronicus*, where Titus is lamenting his, and Lavinia's, woes:

If there were reason for these miseries,
Then into limits could I binde my woes:
When heaven doth weepe, doth not the earth oreflow?
If the windes rage, doth not the Sea wax mad,
Threatning the welkin with his big-swolne face?   5
And wilt thou have a reason for this coile?
I am the Sea. Harke how her sighes doe flow:
Shee is the weeping welkin, I the earth:
Then must my Sea be moved with her sighes,
Then must my earth with her continuall teares,   10

Become a deluge: overflow'd and drown'd:
For why, my bowels cannot hide <u>her</u> woes   (F *Tit* 3.1.219–30)

Theobald (1733) was the first editor to suggest emending 'her' to 'their', to bring it into line with the supposed referent, 'bowels', and recent editions have accepted his identification of 'bowels' as the referent of 'her', but defended the pronoun form as a plural *h*-form. But this is to drag dubious historical linguistics in to defend a simple misreading – the referent of 'her' is not 'bowels', but Lavinia, who is imagined in the passage as weeping so much that Titus, imagined as the earth, overflows, the caves and spaces in the bowels of the earth being full of her tears.

Them/they

As with other nominative/accusative pairs, the accusative form (*them*) can occur in contexts which are nominative:

Your safety: for the which my selfe and <u>them</u>
Bend their best studies   (F *KJ* 4.2.50–1)

Speakers today are still likely to select accusative forms in coordinated pairs like this, even when the pair is in subject position (e.g. 'Billy and <u>me</u> wrote it').

1.3.2g Anomalous pronouns

Type: no man like <u>he</u> doth grieve my heart
          here's none but thee and <u>I</u>
(Abbott, 205, 206, 207, 208, 209, 210, 211, 212, 213, 214, 215, 216, 230)

Abbott's prescriptivist approach, and his interest in illustrating the differences between Early Modern and nineteenth-century English, mean that he spends a long time listing instances of 'anomalous' pronouns. His stance on such forms is made clear by terms like 'misused' and 'ungrammatically' (205). Modern linguists would tend to see variation in pronoun form as part of the natural variation of the language – especially given the long-term shift of English away from case-marking.

English nouns have now lost all case marking. It seems likely that, had all other things been equal, the pronouns would have followed suit, with all pronouns undergoing a similar change to that observed in the second person system, where nominative and accusative forms merge into a single form, *you*. However, all other things were not equal: standardization effectively froze many changes mid-flow, and prescriptivism increased uncertainty in speakers, producing hypercorrection (for example 'She saw Billy and I', where a nominative form is used in an accusative context).

A range of examples from Shakespeare testify to the variation in pronoun form choice in the period, and some of the factors affecting it. (The following sections, dealing with the pronouns *I*, *me*, *thee/thou*, *he*, *him* and *she/her*, duplicate the material on each of these pronouns contained in sections 1.3.2a–c.)

I

Despite being the nominative form, *I* can occur in contexts where we would expect the accusative form (*me*):

O time, thou must untangle this, not I	(F *TN* 2.2.39)

Du. Her husband, sirrah?
Vio. No my Lord, not I   (F *TN* 5.1.143)

We are alone, here's none but thee, & I   (F *2H6* 1.2.69)

all debts are cleerd between you and I   (Fp *MV* 3.2.317)

You know my Father hath no childe, but I   (Fp *AYL* 1.2.16)

Unlesse you would devise some vertuous lye,
To doe more for me then mine owne desert,
And hang more praise upon deceased I   (Q *Son* 72.5–6)

which may make this Island
Thine owne for ever, and I thy *Caliban*
For aye thy foot-licker   (F *Tem* 4.1.216–18)

As with most anomalous forms, Abbott (205) takes a prescriptive view, labelling these instances of neglect or misuse of grammar. However, as was noted in the Overview, it can be argued that case distinctions (such as that between accusative and nominative) have broken down in English – and certainly if this were happening we would expect long-term variation between forms in all contexts. The examples above look like Present-day hypercorrection, but Shakespeare was writing before prescriptivism, so such an explanation is unlikely.

Abbott suggests that euphony may be an element in pronoun choice. The third example above avoids the pairing 'thee and me', and others tend to occur after a dental consonant (while the example from the *Sonnets* is for rhyme). Euphony may be a conditioning factor, but given the variation inherent in the language (and continuing today) we do not need to look any further for an explanation. The most important thing to note is that these are not examples of hypercorrection, nor is Shakespeare putting 'incorrect' forms in the mouths of his characters for stylistic purposes.

Me

Abbott (210) cites the following as examples of *me* used for *I*. However, the fact that the pronouns are clearly in non-subject roles accounts for the use of the accusative form. Most Present-day speakers of British English would find 'I' pedantic or downright ungrammatical in these contexts

| A man no mightier then thy selfe, or <u>me</u> | (F *JC* 1.3.76) |

| Is she as tall as <u>me</u>? | (F *AC* 3.3.11) |

Thee/thou

As stated in the Overview, it can be argued that the case system of Old English is simplified successively in Middle, Early Modern and Present-day English into a binary subject/non-subject system where speakers use the non-subject form as a default, except in cases where the context makes the pronoun unambiguously subject. This explains the tendency for accusative forms to spread generally, and especially for their appearance in post-verbal contexts where their position makes them look non-subject like, whatever a strict application of grammatical rules might imply. Abbott's prescriptivist tendencies thus lead him to worry unduly about imperative instances such as:

| Blossome, speed <u>thee</u> well | (F *WT* 3.3.46) |

| Good Margaret runne <u>thee</u> to the parlour | (F *MA* 3.1.1) |

| Stand <u>thee</u> by Frier | (F *MA* 4.1.22) |

| Hearke <u>thee</u>, a word | (F *Cym* 1.6.32) |

Abbott also worries about contexts after *to be*, where prescriptive rules require nominative forms (for example 'It is <u>I</u>'), but usage almost always supplies accusative, or non-subject forms (for example 'It is <u>me</u>'):

| I would not be <u>thee</u> Nunckle | (Fp *KL* 1.4.182–3) |

Ape. Art thou proud yet?
Tim. I, that I am not <u>thee</u>   (F *Tim* 4.3.277–8)

| it is <u>thee</u> I fear | (F *2H6* 4.1.117) |

He

He, the nominative form, is normally associated with subject roles, but it can crop up in non-subject roles:

'Tis better thee without, then <u>he</u> within   (F *Mac* 3.4.14)

Here, it is perhaps chosen for the sake of euphony with 'thee'. It also occurs in syntactically ambiguous contexts:

Which, of <u>he</u>, or Adrian, for a good wager,
First begins to crow?   (F *Tem* 2.1.28–9)

Here 'he' is the object of the preposition 'of', which might prompt accusative case (*him*), but 'he' is also the subject of 'begins', and occupies clause-initial position – so nominative marking appears. Similarly:

And yet no man like <u>he</u>, doth grieve my heart   (F *RJ* 3.5.83)

where 'like' might be expected to prompt accusative case ('like him'), but 'he' is also the subject of 'doth grieve', and appears before the verb in the clause.

In some contexts where *he* is not clause-initial, it may be selected as more emphatic than *him*:

And were I any thing but what I am,
I would wish me onely <u>he</u>   (F *Cor* 1.1.230–1)

(Though euphony is possibly at work here as well.)

The effect of the pronoun being clause-initial is strong:

Thus <u>he</u> that over-ruld, I over-swayed   (Q *VA* 109)

which could be paraphrased as 'I over-swayed <u>him</u>'. Similarly:

And <u>he</u>, my husband best of all affects   (F *MW* 4.4.86)

That is, 'my husband likes <u>him</u> best'.

Him

In the following instances, the pronouns are the subjects of distant main verbs, but carry the object form because of a closer verb in a relative clause:

<u>Him</u> I accuse:
The City Ports by this hath enter'd   (F *Cor* 5.6.5)

'Him' is the subject of 'hath enter'd' (a rewording would be 'he hath enter'd . . .'), but the pronoun appears in accusative form because the person in question is the object of the relative clause: 'Him (that) I accuse . . .'. The principle of proximity wins out. Similarly:

> I, better then <u>him</u> I am before knowes mee   (Fp *AYL* 1.1.43)

where the main clause is 'he knows me', but the proximity of the relative, 'I am before (him)' triggers the accusative case on 'him'. Also:

> Better to leave undone, then by our deed
> Acquire too high a Fame, when <u>him</u> we serve's away   (F *AC* 3.1.14–15)

She/her

As I have suggested in regard to the other pronouns, there seems to be a general tendency in English for accusative forms to move into all non-subject slots. The feminine singular pronoun behaves slightly differently, however. Abbott notes that *she* is much more likely than *he* to be used as a noun:

> And yet by heaven I thinke my love as rare,
> As any <u>she</u> beli'd with false compare   (Q *Son* 130.13–14)

And *she* often crops up in accusative contexts, indicating that *she*, rather than *her*, may be the default form for speakers:

> Yes, you have seene *Cassio* and <u>she</u> together   (F *Oth* 4.2.3)

> So sawcy with the hand of <u>she</u> heere, what's her name   (F *AC* 3.13.98)

Apparent position can be as important in assigning case as actual grammatical context. In the following, which Abbott found a 'remarkable anomaly' (211), *she* is selected, rather than *her*, because *she* looks like a subject, coming at the start of a relative clause:

> Praise him that got thee, <u>she</u> that gave thee sucke   (F *TC* 2.3.241)

The phonological similarity between *thee* and *she* may also be relevant here.

1.3.2h Reflexive pronouns

Type: myself   thyself
(Abbott, 20, 223)

In Present-day Standard English, reflexive pronouns function either emphatically, occurring in **apposition** with a standard subject pronoun:

> I did it myself
> I myself did it

or as the objects of pronouns in object constructions:

> I'm going to write a note to <u>myself</u>

Such usages occur in Early Modern English, alongside less familiar-looking constructions.

Myself: as subject

For example, Early Modern English allows reflexive forms to appear as full subjects:

> Madame, <u>my selfe</u> have lym'd a Bush for her   (F *2H6* 1.3.89)

where today they could only be used in such contexts as emphatic support to *I* – for example 'I, myself have limed a bush for her'. Similarly:

> <u>My selfe</u> have Letters of the self-same Tenure   (F *JC* 4.3.170)

> <u>My selfe</u> have to mine owne turn'd Enemy   (F *JC* 5.3.2)

Omission of the standard subject pronoun in such contexts may be encouraged by metrical considerations (there are relatively few examples of this in the prose-heavy *Merry Wives of Windsor*), but not all examples are in verse.

A further feature of Early Modern reflexive pronouns is that compositors almost always set the initial pronoun and the *self* element as two separate words (as reproduced here) – not as the compound which actually appears in all modernized texts. Printers did not regularly set reflexive pronouns as a single word until the late seventeenth century. This tendency to treat the two elements of the reflexive pronoun as separate words has a historical basis, since these pronouns are made up of two elements: accusative/dative Middle English pronouns and the Old English derived word *self*.

The orthographic representation of *my self,* and other reflexives, as two words indicates the possibility that the *self* can be considered a different entity from the accompanying pronoun. There are examples of *self* triggering third person agreement:

> Even so my <u>selfe</u> bewayles good *Glosters* case
> With sad unhelpefull teares, and with dimn'd eyes;
> Looke after him   (F *2H6* 3.1.217–19)

> Madam, your <u>selfe</u> <u>is</u> not exempt from this   (F *R3* 2.1.18)

Compare this with the more expected Quarto version:

> Madame your <u>selfe</u> <u>are</u> not exempt in this   (Q *R3* 2.1.18)

Also:

> <u>Is</u> it your <u>selfe</u>?   (F *AW* 3.5.43)

> The Dukes in Counsell, and your Nobleselfe,
> I am sure is sent for   (F *Oth* 1.2.92–3)

As the *OED* notes (*yourself* II 4a), here, 'self' is being analysed as a separate noun phrase.

1.3.2i Dative pronouns (ethical dative)

Type: I am appointed <u>him</u> to murder you
        I made <u>me</u> no more ado

(Abbott, 220)

Old English, at least potentially, preserved a case distinction between accusative (used to mark **direct objects**) and dative (used for several functions, most typically to mark indirect objects). In keeping with the general loss of case distinctions in English, all the morphology associated with marking dative case disappeared from the language during the Old English and Middle English periods. Again in keeping with the general pattern of historical change in English, the functions performed by this lost morphology (marking indirect objects, for example), are now performed by analytic constructions, for example *to him*, *from him*, *by him*. In Early Modern English, however, it is quite common to find bare objective pronouns in positions which in previous states of the language would have called for dative marking, and today would demand prepositional phrases:

> I am appointed <u>him</u> to murther you   (F *WT* 1.2.412)

which means: 'I have been appointed <u>by him</u> to murder you' (I am afraid to say that the Arden 2 editor misunderstands this construction and glosses this line as 'I have been appointed as the person who is to murder you'). Such usages are often termed **ethical dative** forms.

A relic of this usage survives in Present-day English in phrases like 'Give it <u>me</u>' (comparable to 'Give it <u>to me</u>').

Thus we have the following examples:

> Let me remember thee what thou hast promis'd,
> Which is not yet perform'd <u>me</u>   (F *Tem* 1.2.243–4)

That is, 'which is not yet performed <u>for me</u>'.

> give me your present to one Maister
>
> *Bassanio*   (Fp *MV* 2.2.103–4)

That is, 'give your present to Master Bassanio <u>for me</u>'.

> Say'st thou <u>me</u> so   (F *2H6* 2.1.108)

That is, 'Is that what you're saying <u>to me</u>?'

This construction is also used in contexts where the action implied in the verb, although happening to someone or something other than the referent of the pronoun, is perceived as having some effect on the person referred to:

> See, how this River comes <u>me</u> cranking in,
> And cuts <u>me</u> from the best of all my Land,
> A huge halfe Moone   (F *1H4* 3.1.94–6)

Constructions like this are particularly likely to appear in narration, where their use underlines the relevance of the event to one or both of the participants in the conversation, and implies a high degree of emotional involvement in the events narrated:

> he
>
> pluckt <u>me</u> ope his Doublet   (F *JC* 1.2.261–2)

> He presently, as Greatnesse knowes it selfe,
> Steps <u>me</u> a little higher then his Vow   (F *1H4* 4.3.74–5)

In keeping with its association with involved spoken narrative, the construction is informal, though it does not seem to be socially marked, being used by high- and low-status characters.

In some contexts this usage is confusing, since the pronoun can look like a direct object – and Grumio misunderstands it as such in *The Taming of the Shrew*:

> *Petr.*   . . . Heere sirra *Grumio*, knocke I say.
> *Gru.*   Knocke sir? whom should I knocke? Is there
> any man ha's rebus'd your worship?
> *Petr.*   Villaine I say, knocke me heere soundly.
> *Gru.*   Knocke you heere sir? Why sir, what am I sir,
> that I should knocke you heere sir.
> *Petr.*   Villaine I say, knocke me at this gate,
> And rap me well, or Ile knocke your knaues pate.   (Fp *TS* 1.2.5–12)

1.3.2j Pronouns as nouns

Type: two such <u>shes</u>
(Abbott, 224)

Early Modern English allows pronouns more scope to function as if they were full nouns than Present-day English. They can thus take determiners and pre-head modification:

Ile bring mine action on <u>the proudest he</u>
That stops my way in *Padua*   (F *TS* 3.2.232–3)

Lady, you are <u>the cruell'st shee</u> alive   (F *TN* 1.5.244)

            I thinke my love as rare,
As <u>any she</u> beli'd with false compare   (Q *Son* 130.13–14)

<u>That she</u> belov'd, knowes nought, that knowes not this (F *TC* 1.2.293)

and even plural inflections:

two such She's   (F *Cym* 1.7.40)

Early Modern English is also happier to post-modify pronouns with relative clauses than we are today:

            Are not you hee,
That frights the maidens   (F *MND* 2.1.34–5)

which in Present-day English would be: 'Are you not <u>the man</u> that frightens the maidens?'

1.3.3 ADJECTIVES AS HEADS OF NOUN PHRASES

Type: the inconsiderate   the wise
(Abbott, 5)

It is relatively common to find adjectives functioning as the heads of noun phrases, as in this exchange from *Love's Labour's Lost*:

Ar. ... doth <u>the inconsiderate</u> take *salve* for *lenvoy*, and the word *lenvoy* for a *salve*?
Pa. Doe <u>the wise</u> thinke them other   (Fp *LLL* 3.1.74–7)

where 'the inconsiderate' can be taken to mean 'the inconsiderate person', and 'the wise' to mean 'wise people'.

Most such instances can be explained by simple ellipsis as above, but others are more complex:

> a suddain <u>pale</u>,
> Like lawne being spred upon the blushing rose,
> Usurpes her cheeke (Q *VA* 549–51)

> Before these bastard signes of <u>faire</u> were borne (Q *Son* 68.3)

> Till Fortune, tir'd with doing bad,
> Threw him ashore, to give him <u>glad</u> (Q *Per* 2.0.37–8)

In each case here, bare adjectival forms function as noun phrase heads, where Present-day English would require these to take a noun suffix: 'pale<u>ness</u>', 'fair<u>ness</u>', 'glad<u>ness</u>'.

1.3.4 DETERMINERS AS HEADS OF NOUN PHRASES

Type: a <u>many</u> of our bodies
The <u>one</u>
(Abbott, 87, 89, 90)

The use of determiners as the heads of noun phrases produces constructions which can look strange to Present-day speakers:

> In <u>manies</u> lookes, the false hearts history
> Is writ in moods and frounes, and wrinckles strange (Q *Son* 93.7–8)

> *Mor.* How shall I know if I doe choose the right.
> *Por.* <u>The one</u> of them contains my picture Prince (F *MV* 2.7.10–1)

Note that in both of the following cases, 'many' is taken to be singular! This is an indication that in each case the 'many' is considered to be a single collective entity:

> <u>A many</u> of our bodyes shall no doubt
> Find Native Graves (F *H5* 4.3.95–6)

> O thou fond <u>Many</u>, with what loud applause
> Did'st thou beate heaven with blessing *Bullingbrooke* (F *2H4* 1.3.91–2)

See also 1.1.0 for more on determiners as the heads of noun phrases.

1.3.5 -*ING* FORMS AS HEADS OF NOUN PHRASES

Type: You need not fear the <u>having</u> any of these lords
He shall have old <u>turning</u> the key
(Abbott, 93)

Present-day Standard English uses *of* prepositional phrases and the definite article to distinguish between *-ing* forms functioning as nouns:

the having of any of these lords
he shall have old turning of the key

and their use as present participles:

having any of these lords
he shall have turning of the key

In Early Modern English it is common to find *-ing* forms appearing with a definite article (making them look noun-like) but without *of* prepositional phrases (making them look verb-like):

You neede not feare Lady the having any of
these Lords   (Fp *MV* 1.2.96)

Besides, the seeing these effects will be
Both noysome and infectious   (F *Cym* 1.6.25–6)

   Duke.   . . . you are to
do me both a present, and a dangerous courtesie.
   Pro. Pray Sir, in what?
   Duke. In the delaying death   (Fp *MM* 4.2.160–3)

Nothing in his Life became him,
Like the leaving it   (F *Mac* 1.4.7–8)

The invariable misquotation of the final example illustrates the pressure we now feel to use the *of* construction after *-ing* forms in these contexts.

See also 2.1.4 for more on *-ing* forms.

POST-HEAD ELEMENTS

1.4.0 OVERVIEW

The two most frequent post-modifying structures in noun phrases are prepositional phrases (PP) and relative clauses (RC):

NP(a man PP(<u>of vileness</u>))
NP(a man RC(<u>who is vile</u>))

These are the default strategies for post-head modification in English. Prepositional phrases are dealt with in section 1.4.1 and relative clauses in 1.4.2.

Much less frequently, post-head modification involves noun phrases in apposition:

a man, <u>vileness</u>   NP(a man, NP(vileness))

or postpositive adjectival phrases (AP):

a man <u>vile</u>   NP(a man AP(vile))

These structures are marked in English, and tend to be characteristic of poetic or formal language. Noun phrases are dealt with in section 1.4.3, and postpositive adjectival phrases in section 1.4.4.

1.4.1 PREPOSITIONAL PHRASES

Type: such a deal <u>of wonder</u>

Prepositional phrases consist of a governing preposition and a noun phrase object (the following examples all come from *The Winter's Tale* 5.2.20–40, as originally quoted in section 1.0):

such a deale PP(of NP(wonder))

When they function as post-head modification, prepositional phrases are embedded in the noun phrase they modify:

NP(the veritie PP(of it))

NP(The Mantle PP(of Queene Hermiones))

NP(Her Jewell PP(about the neck of it))

Along with predicative placement of adjectives after the verb *to be*, and relative clauses, prepositional phrases represent the unmarked strategy for modifying nouns in English. Of the fifteen modified main nouns in *The Winter's Tale* 5.2.20–40, only four are pre-head modified, while eleven are post-head modified: three have relative clauses, and eight have prepositional phrases.

1.4.2 RELATIVE CLAUSES

Type: my oath which God defend a knight should violate
            the reverent care I bear unto my lord
(Abbott, 244–89)

Relative pronouns and antecedents

Relative clauses function as post-head modification within noun phrases. The most frequent type of relative clause is introduced by a **relative pronoun**, which refers back to the head noun of the modified noun phrase. This head noun is known as the **antecedent**.

The following lines contain three relative clauses:

My name is *Tho. Mowbray*, Duke of Norfolk,
Who hither comes engaged by my oath
(Which heaven defend a knight should violate)
Both to defend my loyalty and truth,
To God, my King, and my succeeding issue,
Against the Duke of Herford that appeales me   (F *R2* 1.3.16–21)

The relatives are:

Thomas Mowbray, Duke of Norfolk, RC(who hither comes)
my oath RC(which God defend a knight should violate)
the Duke of Hereford RC(that appeals me)

The relative pronouns (underlined) are 'who', 'which' and 'that', and their antecedents are '*Tho. Mobray*', 'oath' and 'the Duke of Herford'.

In addition to *who, which* and *that*, there are a number of much less frequent relative pronouns (*as, what, when, where*) and, most significant, *zero*:

The reverent care ^ I beare unto my Lord,
Made me collect these dangers in the Duke   (F *2H6* 3.1.34–5)

which could be rewritten:

The reverent care RC(<u>that</u> I bear unto my lord)
Made me collect these dangers in the Duke

Relative pronouns in Early Modern English often appear to trigger singular agreement on the verb in the relative clause, even though the antecedent is plural:

all things that <u>belongs</u>
To house or house-keeping   (F *TS* 2.1.348–9)

More examples of these constructions will be found in section 1.4.2i, and an explanation of the verb morphology is at 2.1.8a.

Present-day constraints on relative pronouns

In Present-day Standard English, the relative pronouns are constrained in terms of the contexts in which they can appear.

Who appears only with human antecedents:

the man (<u>who</u> knows me)
**the bus* (<u>who</u> takes me into work)

Which appears with non-human antecedents:

**the man* (<u>which</u> knows me)
the bus (<u>which</u> takes me into work)

That is avoided in **non-restrictive relative clauses** – which means a clause where the information supplied by the relative is not essential to identifying the antecedent:

**Suzanne,* (<u>that</u> I live with), teaches in Edinburgh

Here the antecedent is identified by name, and the information in the relative is incidental: Present-day Standard English would require *who* as the pronoun here.

In **restrictive relatives**, where the information is essential to identifying the antecedent, *that* can be used in Present-day Standard English:

the Suzanne (<u>that</u> I live with) teaches in Edinburgh

Here, the information in the relative is essential to distinguishing between two or more people with the name 'Suzanne': hence the relative *restricts* the reference of the noun.

Zero is allowed in Present-day Standard English only if the antecedent is the object of the verb in the relative clause. So

the man (^ I know) lives in Glasgow

is acceptable because the antecedent ('the man') is the object of the relative clause, as the paraphrase 'I know <u>him</u>' shows.

However,

*the man (^ knows me) lives in Glasgow

is not acceptable because the antecedent ('the man') is the subject of the relative clause. Here, the relative clause can be paraphrased '<u>he</u> knows me'.

Such zero subject forms *are* acceptable in many spoken non-standard varieties of Present-day English, however, so you may not find the above example strange.

The relative pronouns in Early Modern English

The Present-day constraints on the use of relatives were slowly forming during the Early Modern period. No writers follow them fully, and individuals vary as to the extent to which they follow the constraints. Amongst the Early Modern London playwrights, Shakespeare's usage of relative pronouns is generally less standardized than most.

Aside from questions of antecedent constraint, the relative pronouns can be distinguished by formality: the *wh-* forms (being newer and associated with writing) are more formal than *that* and *zero* (which are older, and associated with speech).

1.4.2a *Who* relatives

Present-day Standard English allows *who* forms (including *whom*) only with fully human antecedents. In the Early Modern period, it is possible to find *who* used with animals (Abbott, 264):

> Oft have I seene a hot ore-weening Curre,
> Run backe and bite, because he was with-held,
> <u>Who</u> being suffer'd with the Beares fell paw,
> Hath clapt his taile betweene his legges and cride   (F *2H6* 5.1.151–4)

> Against the Capitoll I met a Lyon,
> <u>Who</u> glaz'd upon me, and went surly by   (F *JC* 1.3.20–1)

and also with inanimate nouns:

And thou that smil'dst at good Duke *Humfries* death,
Against the senselesse windes shall grin in vaine,
<u>Who</u> in contempt shall hisse at thee againe   (F *2H6* 4.1.75–7)

Here, as often with inanimate *who*, the inanimate antecedent is being personified by the metaphor. This tendency is also illustrated by the three relative pronouns in the following:

See how the blood is setled in his face.
Oft have I seene a timely-parted Ghost,
Of ashy semblance, meager, pale, and bloodlesse,
Being all descended to the labouring heart,
<u>Who</u> in the Conflict <u>that</u> it holds with death,
Attracts the same for aydance 'gainst the enemy,
<u>Which</u> with the heart there cooles and ne're returneth,
To blush and beautifie the Cheeke againe   (F *2H6* 3.2.159–66)

The language is condensed here, but the relatives are as follows:

The labouring heart RC(<u>who</u> in the conflict . . . attracts the same . . .)
The conflict RC(<u>that</u> it holds with death)
The same . . . RC(<u>which</u> with the heart there cools . . .)

Here, 'heart' attracts the relative pronoun 'who', despite being referred to as 'it' – the heart is personified, in contrast to 'Conflict' and 'same' (i.e. 'blood'), which take pronouns expected with inanimates.

It has been claimed that non-human *who* is a specifically Shakespearean usage, but it can be found in the work of other writers. It is certainly less common than human *which* in Early Modern usage though, and Shakespeare does use non-human *who* at a higher rate than other writers.

1.4.2b *Which* relatives

Which can occur easily with human antecedents, even fully named ones:

For that *John Mortimer*, <u>which</u> now is dead,
In face, in gate, in speech he doth resemble   (F *2H6* 3.1.372–3)

Here the fact that Mortimer is dead may assist the use of 'which'.

Which is the relative most frequently found acting as a **sentential relative**, where it has as its antecedent not a noun phrase, but a whole clause (I have italicized the antecedents in the following):

> But there are other strict observances:
> As *not to see a woman in that terme,*
> <u>Which</u> I hope well is not enrolled there.
> And *one day in a week to touch no foode:*
> And *but one meale on every day beside:*   5
> <u>The which</u> I hope is not enrolled there.
> And *then to sleepe but three houres in the night,*
> And *not be seene to winke of all the day.*
> When I was wont to thinke no harme all night,
> And make a darke night too of halfe the day: 10
> <u>Which</u> I hope well is not enrolled there   (F *LLL* 1.1.36–46)

Here the antecedents are the 'strict observances' which the young men try to live by, and the passage illustrates the variation found in the period between *which* and *the which* for sentential relatives.

1.4.2c *That* relatives

That is much more likely to occur in non-restrictive relatives in the Early Modern period than today:

> Let *Fame*, <u>that</u> all hunt after in their lives,
> Live registred upon our brazen Tombes   (F *LLL* 1.1.1–2)

Here, the information in the relative is not essential to identifying the head, so the relative is non-restrictive, and in Present-day English would tend to take *which*. The relative here would only become restrictive if the speaker were trying to distinguish between different types of fame – but the bare noun '*Fame*' implies that fame in a general sense is intended.

Just a few lines later we do get a restrictive relative in a similar construction:

> That honour <u>which</u> shall bate his sythes keene edge,
> And make us heyres of all eternitie   (F *LLL* 1.1.6–7)

Here the relative is restrictive in that the honour envisaged is a specific type of honour.

1.4.2d *Zero* relatives

As in Present-day English, *zero* relative pronouns can appear when the antecedent noun is the object of the verb in the relative clause:

> The reverent care ^ I beare unto my Lord
> Made me collect these dangers in the Duke   (F *2H6* 3.1.34–5)

That is, 'The reverent *care* [which/that] I bear unto my lord'. The paraphrase of the relative clause – 'I bear the care' – shows that the antecedent of the *zero* pronoun is the object of 'bear'.

Early Modern English is much more likely than Present-day Standard English to allow *zero* relative pronouns where the antecedent noun is the subject of the verb in the relative clause:

> First note, that he is neere you in discent,
> And should you fall, he is the next ^ will mount   (F *2H6* 3.1.21–2)

That is, 'he is the *next* [who/that] will mount'. The paraphrase of the relative clause – 'the next will mount' – shows that the antecedent of the *zero* pronoun is the subject of 'will mount'.

Zero relatives are frequently used after demonstrative *that*, possibly as a way of avoiding 'that that' combinations:

> Thy Honorable Mettle may be wrought
> From that ^ it is dispos'd   (F *JC* 1.2.306–7)

That is, 'From that [which/that] it is disposed [to]'.

1.4.2e Relative pronoun/conjunctive *but*

Type: there is no man but hates me
(Abbott, 123)

In certain constructions, *but* can look very like a relative pronoun:

> and not the least of these,
> But can doe more in England then the King   (F *2H6* 1.3.70–1)

> There is no voice so simple, but assumes
> Some marke of vertue on his outward parts   (F *MV* 3.2.81–2)

which could be analysed as follows:

> ?the least of these RC(but can do more . . .)
> ?no voice is so simple RC(but assumes some mark of virtue . . .)

However, examples such as the following:

> I found no man, but he was true to me   (F *JC* 5.5.35)

> There's nere a villaine dwelling in all Denmarke
> But hee's an arrant knave   (F *Ham* 1.5.129–30)

where *but* is accompanied by an explicit subject ('but he . . .'), suggest that *but* does not have pronominal function, and that we should analyse the apparently subjectless examples as having a *zero* pronoun:

> not the least of these but (he) can do more in England than the King

These uses of *but* are best seen as conjunctive – joining two clauses, with frequent ellipsis of a second subject.

1.4.2f Determiners as antecedents of relatives

Type: In his way that comes in triumph
(Abbott, 218)

Occasionally, constructions are found where the relative pronoun has as its antecedent a possessive determiner rather than the head noun of the noun phrase it modifies. For example:

> in his way,
> That comes in Triumph over *Pompeyes* blood   (F *JC* 1.1.50–1)

where the antecedent of the relative pronoun 'that' is 'his' rather than the expected 'way'. Clearly, semantics overrides strict grammatical logic here: the referent of 'his' (Caesar) is more important than the route he takes. Similarly:

> Love make his heart of flint, that you shal love   (F *TN* 1.5.290)

where the antecedent of 'that' is 'his', rather than the head noun 'heart'. Similar constructions occur in

> If you had knowne the vertue of the Ring,
> Or halfe her worthinesse that gave the Ring   (F *MV* 5.1.199–200)

and

> they shall strike
> *Your* Children yet unborne, and unbegot,
> *That* lift your Vassall Hands against my Head.   (F *R2* 3.2.86–8)

1.4.2g Head-shifted relatives

Type: This island's mine by Sycorax my mother which thou tak'st
          from me

The vast majority of relative clauses in Present-day English have the following structure:

NP(HEAD RC(. . .))

where the relative clause is part of the noun phrase it modifies, and functions with it in clause structure (VP = verb phrase):

NP(This island RC(which thou tak'st from me)) VP(is) Co(mine)

Early Modern English allowed a looser relationship between the modified noun phrase and the relative clause, with the result that other elements of clause structure can often be found separating the two:

> This Island's mine by *Sycorax* my mother,
> Which thou tak'st from me   (F *Tem* 1.2.333–4)

Here, the relative clause, 'Which thou tak'st from me', modifies 'Island', but has been moved out of the noun phrase and placed at the end of the clause after the verb ('is') and the complement ('mine'):

NP(This island ^) VP(s) COMP(mine) ADV(by Sycorax my mother) RC(which thou tak'st from me)

Present-day Standard written English resists this movement of the relative away from the head (what I am calling 'head-shifting'), though it is possible to hear such structures in spoken English, where intonation can be used to avoid possible ambiguity about the antecedent of the relative pronoun.

Such head-shifted relatives are not hard to find in Shakespeare:

> Why should hee stay, whom Love doth press to go?   (F *MND* 3.2.184)

> You (my Lord) best know
> (Whom least will seeme to doe so) my past life   (F *WT* 3.2.31)

> What private greefes they have, alas I know not,
> That made them do it   (F *JC* 3.2.215–16)

> Old Lord, I cannot blame thee,
> Who, am my selfe attach'd with wearinesse
> To th'dulling of my spirits: Sit downe, and rest:
> Even here I will put off my hope, and keepe it
> No longer for my Flatterer: he is drown'd
> Whom thus we stray to finde   (F *Tem* 3.3.4–9)

1.4.2h Headless relatives

Type: I cannot justify whom the law condemns

In extreme instances, relatives can appear without an antecedent head noun:

> I cannot justifie whom the Law condemnes   (F *2H6* 2.3.16)

Here, the entire relative functions as the object of 'justifie':

NP(I) VP(cannot justifie) RC(whom the Law condemnes)

1.4.2i Relative pronouns and verb agreement

Type: all things that <u>belongs</u> to house and house-keeping
(Abbott, 247)

It is very common in Early Modern English to find instances where relative markers with plural antecedents apparently trigger singular agreement on the verb in the relative clause, producing -*s* or -*th* inflection:

all things that <u>belongs</u>

To house or house-keeping   (F *TS* 2.1.348–9)

Contagious fogges: Which falling in the Land,
<u>Hath</u> evrie pettie River made so proud   (F *MND* 2.1.90–1)

   Troy. Well know they what they speak that <u>speakes</u>
so wisely   (F *TC* 3.2.150)

they laugh that <u>winnes</u>   (F *Oth* 4.1.121)

In fact, as I argue in section 2.1.8a, these are plural inflections, remnants of earlier systems surviving in Early Modern as part of something called the Northern Personal Pronoun Rule (or *they* constraint). The older inflections tend not to occur when the verb is next to the pronoun *they* (note the variation in the example from *Troilus and Cressida*), and seem to be more likely to occur when their immediate subject is a relative pronoun.

1.4.3 NOUN PHRASES AS POST-HEAD MODIFICATION (APPOSITION)

Type: Sycorax, <u>my mother</u>
            you, <u>my Lord</u>

Apposition is the simple placement of two equivalent grammatical structures next to each other. It is most frequently found with noun phrases, as in the following example, where the two noun phrases share a grammatical role (complement of 'is') and effectively modify each other. It is of course a moot, not to say pointless, question whether we are dealing with pre- or post-head modification here:

My name is <u>*Tho. Mowbray*</u>, <u>Duke of Norfolk</u>,
Who hither comes engaged by my oath   (F *R2* 1.3.16–17)

Similarly:

This Island's mine by *Sycorax* <u>my mother</u>,
Which thou tak'st from me   (F *Tem* 1.2.333–4)

<u>You (my Lord)</u> best know
(Whom least will seeme to doe so) my past life   (F *WT* 3.2.31)

1.4.4 POSTPOSITIVE ADJECTIVAL PHRASES

Type: heir <u>apparent</u>
          creatures <u>vile</u>
(Abbott, 419, 419a)

Adjectives can occur immediately after the noun they modify for a number of reasons. Frequently, *noun + adjective* order is triggered when the noun is derived from French or the phrase has been influenced by legal French (since noun + adjective is the normal order in French):

             were it not heere apparant,
that thou art Heire <u>apparant</u>   (Fp *1H4* 1.2.55–6)

thou cam'st not of the blood-<u>royall</u>   (Fp *1H4* 1.2.136)

Or whether that the body <u>publique</u>, be
          A horse   (F *MM* 1.2.149–50)

Elsewhere, postposition of the adjective is usually an attempt to emphasize the adjective rather than the noun:

In killing Creatures <u>vilde</u>, as Cats and Dogges   (F *Cym* 5.5.252)

             Our spoyles he kickt at,
And look'd upon things <u>precious</u>, as they were
The common Muck of the World   (F *Cor* 2.2.124–6)

And this can be seen most clearly in attributive–postpositional pairs, where the attributive adjective is conventional, and the postpositional one is marked in some way:

Celestiall *Dian*, Goddesse *Argentine*   (Q *Per* 5.1.247)

where attributive 'Celestial' is hardly a surprising attribute of the goddess Diana, but postpositional 'argentine' (referring to her associations with the moon, and her silver bow) needs to be worked at.

PART 2

THE VERB PHRASE

OVERVIEW: THE STYLISTICS OF THE VERB PHRASE

Verbs are concerned with actions, processes and states. As such, they usually have people or things who 'do' or experience them (**agents**), relative times of commencement (**tense**), and relative states of completion (**aspect**). *Agency*, *tense* and *aspect* are defined technically in section 2.0b. This first overview section illustrates some of the stylistic potential of verb phrases by looking at scene 2.3 from *Othello*.

This scene marks the point at which Iago first begins to take control of Othello's perceptions. Cassio has been promoted over Iago's head by Othello, and Iago's plan is to discredit Cassio by getting him drunk and provoking a fight:

> *Iago.* If I can fasten but one Cup upon him
> With that which he hath drunke to night alreadie,
> He'l be as full of Quarrell, and offence
> As my yong Mistris dogge.
> Now my sicke Foole *Rodorigo*,   5
> Whom Love hath turn'd almost the wrong side out,
> To *Desdemona* hath tonight Carrows'd.
> Potations, pottle-deepe; and he's to watch.
> Three else of Cyprus, Noble swelling Spirites,
> (That hold their Honours in a wary distance,   10
> The very Elements of this Warrelike Isle)
> Have I to night fluster'd with flowing Cups,
> And they Watch too.
> Now 'mongst this Flocke of drunkards
> Am I [to put] our *Cassio* in some Action   15
> That may offend the Isle.   (F *Oth* 2.3.44–57)

Iago's plan is successful in provoking a fight. His real triumph, however, lies in the way in which he narrates the events of the fight to Othello, and the subtle implications he makes about agency, and therefore blame. Shakespeare has Iago tell the story of the fight twice, producing a sense of confusion and uncertainty. The first narrative is brief, apparently forced from an unwilling and dazed Iago:

> [*Othello*]   Honest *Iago* that lookes dead with greeving,
> Speake: who began this? On thy love I charge thee?
>   *Iago.*   I do not know: Friends all, but now, even now
> In Quarter, and in termes like Bride, and Groome
> Devesting them for Bed: and then, but now: 5
> (As if some Planet had unwitted men)
> Swords out, and tilting one at others breastes,
> In opposition bloody. I cannot speake
> Any begining to this peevish oddes.
> And would, in Action glorious, I had lost   10
> Those legges, that brought me to a part of it   (F *Oth* 2.3.168–78)

Iago's grammar here represents his supposed confusion through the use of **sentence fragments**, which frequently omit the agent and the tensed verb (omitted elements are given in brackets):

(They were) friends all, but now, even now . . .
(They were) in quarter, and in terms . . .
(They had their) swords out . . .
(They were) tilting one at other's breasts . . .

By omitting agents (the source of the action of the verb) and tensed verbs (which locate an action in time relative to the narrator), Iago introduces a lack of specificity to the narrative. He is anxious not to directly accuse Cassio of anything, and his grammar presents him as an involved but impartial observer, simply relaying impressions. His use of **non-finite verb** forms (see section 2.1.6) such as 'Devesting' and 'tilting', which lack overt subjects and are ambiguous as to tense, aids him in this. Where he does refer explicitly to time, he uses **deictic** terms rather than verb tense: 'now', 'even now', 'and then, but now' and his narrative seems to flicker unsteadily between present-time, as-it-happens, narrative ('now'), and a more considered, more normal, past time ('then').

Finally, in keeping with the suppression of agents early in the passage, Iago ends with a curious construction which has him passively brought to the fight by the intentional motivation of his legs ('Those legges, that brought me to a part of it'). Thus a whole series of stylistic devices cover up Iago's own agency in provoking the fight.

Similarly disruptive techniques are used later in the scene when Iago narrates the fight for a second time. Once again, tenses slide across the surface of the narrative:

This it is Generall:
Montano and my selfe being in speech,
There comes a Fellow, crying out for helpe,
And *Cassio* following him with determin'd Sword
To execute upon him. Sir, this Gentleman,   5
Steppes in to *Cassio*, and entreats his pause:
My selfe, the crying Fellow did pursue,
Least by his clamour (as it so fell out)
The Towne might fall in fright. He, (swift of foote)
Out-ran my purpose: and I return'd then rather   10
For that I heard the clinke, and fall of Swords,
And *Cassio* high in oath: Which till to night
I nere might say before. When I came backe
(For this was briefe) I found them close together
At blow, and thrust, even as againe they were   15
When you your selfe did part them.
More of this matter cannot I report   (F *Oth* 2.3.215–31)

The narration begins and ends with **discourse-marking** present-tense verbs referring to present time: 'This it is_ Generall' and 'More of this matter cannot_ I report'. I call these verbs discourse markers here because they are being used to signal the start and end of the narration within Iago's overall speech. Thus they mark off a significantly differ-ent section of discourse. Away from these points of stability, the rela-tionship between tense and time is less predictable. The narrated events all happened in the past, but the initial ones are presented in the *pres-ent* tense ('comes', 'Steppes', 'entreats'). Then the narrative shifts to past tense at line ('did pursue', 'out-ran', 'return'd', 'heard', 'came', 'found', 'were', 'did part'). As in the first narrative, there are non-finite forms ('being', 'crying', 'following'), although here the agents are explicit ('*Montano* and my selfe', 'a Fellow', '*Cassio*').

The initial **present-for-past narration** maintains the sense that Iago has hardly been able to distance himself from events – that he can barely make sense of what has happened. The shift into **past-for-past narration** at line 7 is marked by the use of an auxiliary *do* form (see sec-tion 2.1.1b): 'My selfe, the crying Fellow did pursue' – and this use is echoed at the end of the narrative when Iago makes reference to Othello: 'When you your selfe did_ part them'. Like the present-for-present forms which frame the narrative, these auxiliary *do* forms seem to serve a discourse-marking function: they mark the beginning and end of the past-for-past narrative. But they also serve to make a parallel between Iago and Othello, since the verb Iago 'does' ('did pursue') is paralleled with the verb Othello does ('did part'). Iago manipulates the structural potential of Early Modern verb phrases to imply a parallel between himself and Othello: to imply that their points of view are the same, and to prepare the way for his more sinister manipulation of Othello's perceptions later in the play.

OVERVIEW: THE STRUCTURE OF THE VERB PHRASE

For the sake of descriptive simplicity, I take the **verb phrase** to include everything in a clause aside from the subject:

Subject	Predicate
I	take it most unkindly
Noun phrase	Verb phrase

Verb phrases have the following idealized structure:

(auxiliary verb) (main verb) (direct object) (indirect object) (complement) (adverbial)
[————HEAD————]

The **main verb,** and an optional **auxiliary verb** or verbs, function together as the head of the verb phrase. All other elements are optional:

Subject	AuxV	MainV	DObj	IObj	Comp	Adv
I	might	give	it	to him		later
She		is			rich	
Paul		cried				
The castle		seemed			pleasant	to them
		Run!				

The idealized structure presented here misrepresents reality to some extent. **Adverbial elements,** for example, are highly mobile, and can easily appear outside the verb phrase before the subject at the start of a clause:

Later I might give it to him
To them, the castle seemed pleasant

Poetic Early Modern English allows the inversion of clause elements relatively easily, which can result in objects and complements moving out of the verb phrase as well:

It to him I might give
Rich she is

These misrepresentations of actual verb phrase structures are a small price to pay for a clear base from which to begin description, and in this overview, and in the detailed sections which follow, I consider each element in turn. I consider first the head of the verb phrase (auxiliary and main verb), and the features marked on it: **tense** and time, **aspect**, **mood**, **voice**, **morphology** and **negation**. I then move on to consider elements of the verb phrase beyond the head: **direct** and **indirect objects**, **complements** and **adverbials**. I will draw most of my examples from the following passage, which consists of the first thirty-eight lines of *Othello*. I have underlined verb phrase heads, and bracketed those where the features of the head are separated

<u>Enter</u> Rodorigo, and Iago.

Rodorigo.

<u>Never tell</u> me, I <u>take</u> it much unkindly
That thou (*Iago*) who <u>hast had</u> my purse,
As if yᵉ strings <u>were</u> thine, <u>should'st know</u> of this.
    Ia. But you<u>'l not heare</u> me. If ever I <u>did dream</u>
Of such a matter, <u>abhorre</u> me.   5
    Rodo. Thou <u>told'st</u> me,
Thou <u>did'st hold</u> him in thy hate.
    Iago. <u>Despise</u> me
If I <u>do not</u>. Three Great-ones of the Cittie,
(In personall suite <u>to make</u> me his Lieutenant)   10
<u>Off-capt</u> to him: and by the faith of man
I <u>know</u> my price, I <u>am</u> worth no worsse a place.
But he (as <u>loving</u> his owne pride, and purposes)
<u>Evades</u> them, with a bumbast Circumstance,
Horribly <u>stufft</u> with Epithites of warre,   15
<u>Non-suites</u> my Mediators. For certes, <u>saies</u> he,
I [<u>have</u> already <u>chose</u>] my Officer. And what <u>was</u> he?
For-sooth, a great Arithmatician,
One *Michaell Cassio*, a *Florentine*,
(A Fellow almost <u>damn'd</u> in a faire Wife)   20
That <u>never set</u> a Squadron in the Field,
[<u>Nor</u> the devision of a Battaile <u>knowes</u>]
More than a Spinster. Unlesse the Bookish Theoricke:
Wherein the Tongued Consuls <u>can propose</u>
As Masterly as he. Meere pratle (without practise)   25
<u>Is</u> all his Souldiership. But he (Sir) <u>had</u> th'election;
And I (of whom his eies <u>had seene</u> the proofe
At Rhodes, at Ciprus, and on others grounds

Christen'd, and Heathen) <u>must be be-leed, and calm'd</u>
By Debitor and Creditor. This Counter-caster,   30
He (in good time) [<u>must</u> his Lieutenant <u>be</u>],
And I (<u>blesse</u> the marke) his Mooreships Auntient.
   Rod. By heaven, I rather <u>would have bin</u> his hang man.
   Iago. Why, there'<u>s</u> no remedie.
'T<u>is</u> the cursse of Service;   35
Preferment <u>goes</u> by Letter, and affection,
And not by old gradation, where each second
<u>Stood</u> Heire to'th'first.   [F *Oth* 1.1.1–38]

THE HEAD

Auxiliary and main (lexical) verbs

As indicated, the auxiliary (if present) and main verb constitute the head of the verb phrase. **Main verbs** are drawn from the set of English **lexical verbs**, and show considerable scope for morphological changes which mark person and number agreement, tense, aspect and mood (see sections 2.1.3–5). **Auxiliary verbs** are drawn from the much more restricted set of **modal** and full auxiliary verbs, and show relatively little morphological change. They are involved in marking modality, **tense**, **aspect** and **voice**, and in the formation of *questions* and *negatives*.

A lexical verb is so called because it carries lexical, or semantic, content as well as the grammatical information associated with verbs (tense, aspect, number agreement, and so on). For example, in the following,

   I (<u>take</u> it much unkindly)

'take' is a lexical verb, which can be analysed as having the semantic content 'feel' or 'react to', as well as carrying the grammatical information 'present tense'. When necessary in description, such elements are represented by a **morphemic level gloss**, as follows:

   I   (<u>take</u>   it much unkindly)
          feel + *present tense*

This can be compared with the sentence

   I   (<u>took</u>   it much unkindly)
          feel + *past tense*

where the semantic content remains the same, but the morphological change indicates the shift in the grammatical meaning of the verb to 'past tense'.

The lexical *and* grammatical function of 'take' or 'took' in these examples can be contrasted with the separation of these functions in 'did'st' and 'hold' in the following:

Thou (<u>did'st hold</u> him in thy hate)

Here, 'hold' is a lexical verb, carrying the semantic content 'have' or 'maintain', but the grammatical information about tense, and second person singular agreement, is carried by the auxiliary verb 'did'st', which has no lexical content at all:

Thou	(did	'st	hold	him in thy hate)
	past tense	*2nd person singular*	maintain	

The set of auxiliary verbs in English includes *be* and *have*, which are used in marking *tense*, *voice* and *aspect*, and the modals, *can*, *may*, *should*, *would*. The main auxiliaries, *do*, *be* and *have*, generally lack any kind of **semantic colouring**, while the modal auxiliaries, as their name implies, carry semantic content which modifies the main verb.

Main and modal auxiliary verbs are covered more fully in sections 2.1.1–2.

Tense and time

Of all the linguistic features involved in verb phrase structure, tense might appear to be the most conceptually simple: **present, past** and **future tenses** are used to refer to times located in relation to the speaker or writer at the time of production. In the extract from *Othello*, when Rodorigo says

I <u>take</u> it much unkindly . . .   (line 1)

he refers to his own present time, using the *simple present tense* form of the verb *to take*. Later when he says

Thou <u>told'st</u> me . . .   (line 6)

he uses the *simple past tense* form of the verb *to tell* to refer to the past. However, when Iago uses a future tense at line 4:

But you'l not heare me

he is not making a prediction about what will happen ('At some point in the future you will not be able to hear me'), but is commenting on something that *is* happening ('You are not listening to me properly').

So something that has the formal properties of a future-tense verb phrase is being used to talk about the present.

Later, in his narrative of Othello meeting the 'Three Great-ones of the Cittie' who plead Iago's case, Iago first uses past tense for past time:

[They] <u>Off-capt</u> to him   (line 11)

but then switches tense, without switching his time-reference, using present tense for past time:

But he . . . <u>Evades</u> them   (lines 13–14)

Clearly, then, there is no simple one-to-one relationship between tense and time-reference: the same tense can refer to different times, and the same time can be referred to by different tenses.

Tense and time are covered more fully in section 2.1.3.

Aspect: perfect and progressive

Along with tense, verb phrases in English can be marked for **aspect**. Aspect has to do with whether or not something has been completed. **Perfect aspect** is applied to states or actions completed in the past; **progressive aspect** is applied to states or actions which are seen as unfinished in some way. Thus when Othello is quoted by Iago as saying

I have already chose my officer   (line 17)

the verb phrase carries perfect aspect, because the choice has been made – the action is completed. The past participle, 'chose', is what marks the verb phrase as perfect. In Present-day Standard English it would be 'chosen' (which is indeed what the Quarto text has here): see section 2.1.4. It would be possible to change the aspect to progressive:

I have already been <u>choosing</u> my officer

where the use of the present participle ('choosing') implies that the action is not yet completed.

Aspect is covered more fully in section 2.1.4.

Mood

English verbs can carry one of three moods: indicative, subjunctive or imperative. **Indicative** verbs refer to events or processes the speaker conceives of as actual, be they past, present or future. **Subjunctive** verbs refer to events or processes the speaker conceives of as hypothetical or contingent in some way, hence:

> If Consequence <u>do</u> but approve my dreame   (F *Oth* 2.3.58)

where subjunctive mood is marked by the lack of person agreement on 'do': compare 'If consequence <u>does</u> but approve my dream'.

The **imperative** mood is used for orders, and, like the subjunctive, consists of the **base form** of the verb (in other words, the **infinitive** without *to*):

> Honest Iago that lookes dead with greeving,
> <u>Speake</u>: who began this?   (F *Oth* 2.3.168–9)

Early Modern English is slightly more likely than Present-day English to have an explicit subject with imperatives (as is found in the previous example), but the most frequent pattern conforms to that of Present-day usage:

> <u>Use</u> me but as your spaniell; <u>spurne</u> me, <u>strike</u> me,
> <u>Neglect</u> me, <u>lose</u> me   (F *MND* 2.1.205–6)

Mood is covered more fully in section 2.1.5.

Finite versus non-finite

A **finite verb** is one which is marked for tense and person agreement; hence the term finite, since these features are held to limit the scope of the verb. In

> But he (as loving his owne pride, and purposes)
> Evades them   (F *Oth* 1.1.12–13)

'Evades' is a finite main verb marked with third person singular, present tense agreement (compare 'they evaded', 'I evade', and so on).

In the same sentence, 'loving' is a **non-finite verb**, since it does not carry person or tense agreement:

> I (as <u>loving</u> my own pride and purposes) evaded them
> they (as <u>loving</u> their own pride and purposes) will evade them

There are three parts of the verb which are non-finite: the **to infinitive**, the **-*ing* form** and the **-*en* form**:

> I (<u>to love</u> my own pride and purposes) evaded them
> I (<u>fearing</u> for my own pride and purposes) evaded them
> I (<u>given</u> my own pride and purposes) evaded them

Finite versus non-finite verbs are covered more fully in section 2.1.6.

Voice: active/passive, agency

Verb phrases can be **active** or **passive**. In an active verb phrase, the entity performing or experiencing the verb (the **agent**) is in the subject position:

subject		object
I	know	my price
agent		

In a passive verb phrase, however, the agent is in the object position, and the grammatical subject (the noun phrase with which the verb agrees) is the entity which has the verb 'done' to it.

subject		object
My price	is known	to me
		agent

Passive verb phrases are formed by adding part of *to be* to the *-en* form of the verb:

active	passive	
I <u>know</u> my price	my price	<u>is known</u> to me
		<u>was known</u> to me
		<u>will be known</u> to me

Active and passive verbs are covered more fully in section 2.1.7.

Verb morphology

In keeping with the general reduction in inflections as English has shifted from being a synthetic to an inflected language, the verb morphology of Present-day Standard English is highly simplified compared to that of Old or Middle English. As in many other things, verb morphology in the Early Modern period represents a late transitional stage: the Present-day system is more or less in place, but uncompleted changes allow for some significant variation.

Present tense morphology

In Present-day Standard English, there is only one remaining verb inflection in the present tense: *-s* on the third person singular.

I tell	we tell
you tell	you tell
he/she/it <u>tells</u>	they tell

In all other persons, the base form of the verb is used.

Early Modern English was not far away from the Present-day system, but retained a separate second person singular inflection for thou (*-est*), and an alternative third person singular inflection (*-eth*):

I tell	we tell
thou tell'st	you tell
you tell	
he/she/it tells	they tell
he/she/it telleth	

These variants are discussed in section 2.1.8a.

Past tense morphology

Most English verbs form their simple past tense by adding *-ed* to the base form:

present	*past*
I walk	I walk<u>ed</u>
she walks	she walk<u>ed</u>

There is no person or number marking in the past tense.

A significant minority of verbs (often frequently occurring ones) form their past tense by altering their central vowel:

present	*past*
I take	I <u>took</u>
she does	she <u>did</u>
we tell	we <u>told</u>

These verbs are known as **strong verbs**, and *-ed* verbs are known as **weak verbs**.

All new verbs in English automatically follow the weak verbs in forming their past tenses (thus 'I googl<u>ed</u> him' – 'I looked him up on Google.com'), but over the history of English there has been movement both ways between the strong and weak classes, evidenced by variation in the Early Modern period which is further considered in section 2.1.8b.

Future tense morphology

Strictly speaking, there is no future tense verb morphology in English, since English futures are formed by an analytic construction adding an auxiliary verb (usually *will*) to the base form of the verb:

present	*future*
she takes	she will take

Variation between *shall* and *will* in future tense formation is considered in section 2.1.2e.

Negation

Negation can be realized by a number of elements, and can appear in a number of different positions in the verb phrase.

The exemplary passage from *Othello* shows several of the possible forms of negation:

adverbial – where an adverbial element is added to the verb phrase to negate the verb:

> Never tell me   (F *Oth* 1.1.1)

> That never set a Squadron in the Field,
> Nor the devision of a Battaile knowes   (F *Oth* 1.1.22–3)

morphological – where a negative affix is added to a word to negate its semantic content:

> I take it much unkindly   (F *Oth* 1.1.1)

> [He] Non-suites my Mediators   (F *Oth* 1.1.16)

grammatical – where a negative particle is added to the verb phrase to negate the verb:

> But you'l not heare me   (F *Oth* 1.1.4)

> If I do not   (F *Oth* 1.1.8)

or by adding a negative determiner to a noun phrase:

> I am worth no worsse a place   (F *Oth* 1.1.11)

> Why, there's no remedie   (F *Oth* 1.1.35)

As with possession (see section 1.1.4), the means to express this feature cross grammatical categories and semantic fields.

Negation is covered more fully in section 2.1.9.

ELEMENTS OF THE VERB PHRASE BEYOND THE HEAD

Subjects and agents

Strictly speaking, the *subject* lies outside the verb phrase altogether:

subject	verb phrase
(Thou)	told'st me thou did'st hold him in thy hate

but there is a close grammatical relationship between the subject and the tensed verb, which must agree with it in terms of person and number.

In an active clause, the subject and agent will be the same:

subject		object
I	saw	him
agent		

but in a passive clause, the agent is the grammatical object:

subject		object
He	was seen	by me
		agent

Subjects and agents are covered more fully in section 2.2.1.

Objects: direct and indirect

While most verbs take only one object, some verbs allow or require two objects, which behave slightly differently from each other, and are termed **direct** and **indirect objects**:

	direct object	indirect object
Thou told'st	(me)	(thou did'st hold him in thy hate)

The direct object is 'me', a pronoun noun phrase; the indirect object is 'thou did'st hold him in thy hate', a noun clause. We can check this by substituting 'it' for the whole of this clause:

Thou told'st (me) (it)

Direct and indirect objects behave differently in a number of ways. Generally, when their positions are reversed, the indirect object will take a preposition such as *to*:

Thou told'st (it) (to me)

and indirect objects are usually easier to delete than direct objects (though this instance is not a very good example of this):

Thou told'st (it)
?Thou told'st (me)

Direct and indirect objects are covered more fully in section 2.2.2.

Complements

The role of **complement** can be realized either by an adjectival phrase or by a noun phrase:

> As if the strings were <u>thine</u>   *possessive adjective*
> <u>Mere prattle without practice</u> is all his soldiership *noun phrase*

Complements differ from objects in their relationship to the subject of the clause. Where objects tend to be different entities from the subject of their clause, complements tend to be identical with, or attributes of, the subject. A fairly restricted set of verbs take complements: *to be, to seem, to become* are the main ones.

Complements are covered more fully in section 2.2.3.

Adverbials

The role of **adverbial** is most commonly realized by **adverbial phrases**, **adverbial clauses** or prepositional phrases:

> I take it <u>much unkindly</u>   *adverbial phrase*
> Thou who hast had my purse <u>as if the strings</u>
>   <u>were thine</u>   *adverbial clause*
> He evades them <u>with a bombast circumstance</u>   *prepositional phrase*

Adverbials are optional – they can normally be deleted easily:

> I take it
> Thou who hast had my purse
> He evades them

and they can usually be moved quite freely within and even beyond the verb phrase:

> much unkindly I take it
> Thou who as if the strings were thine hast had my purse
> He with a bombast circumstance evades them

THE VERB PHRASE HEAD

The head of the verb phrase consists of an optional auxiliary or modal verb, and an obligatory main verb:

subject		—————————————— *verb phrase* ——————————————		
		—————————————— *head* ——————————		
	modal verb	*auxiliary verb(s)*	*main verb*	
I			take	it much unkindly
who		hast	had	my purse
thou	should'st		know	of this
I		did	dream	of such a matter
I		was being	seen	by the doctor
I	must	be	beleed	by him

Modal verbs, as their name implies, modify the meaning of the main verb – usually expressing concepts such as ability (*can*), permission (*may*), and obligation (*must*):

She	<u>can</u>	be	seen
She	<u>must</u>	be	seen

but they are also involved in expressing conditionality (*might, would*):

They	<u>might</u>	come	
thou	<u>should'st</u>	know	of this

In contrast, auxiliary verbs lack this semantic colouring: they are involved in expressing grammatical information by marking tense (for example *have*) and forming passive clauses (*be*):

I	<u>hadn't</u>	met	him then
I	<u>have</u>	met	him
I	<u>was</u>	shown	the painting

Modal and auxiliary verbs have a role in question formation where they swap places with the subject or are introduced to mark the utterance as a question:

| I <u>have</u> met him | → | <u>Have</u> I met him? |
| I met him | → | <u>Did</u> I meet him? |

Main verbs carry the semantic content of the verb phrase and, if there is no auxiliary or modal verb, can be marked for tense and number agreement.

The auxiliary and modal verbs developed out of main verbs in the Old and Middle English periods. In some cases, two forms of the verb still survive – so *do* and *have* exist in auxiliary and main verb forms:

main verb	She <u>did</u> it
auxiliary	<u>Did</u> she write that novel?
main verb	I <u>have</u> it
auxiliary	I <u>have</u> got it

Note here that 'did' in 'She did it' has the semantic content 'perform', whereas 'Did' in 'Did she write that novel' has a purely grammatical function, marking the sentence as a question, and carrying tense; the semantic content here is found on 'write'. Similarly, in 'I have it', 'have' carries semantic *and* grammatical information ('possess' and 'first person present tense' respectively), while in 'I have got it', the semantic information has moved to 'got', leaving 'have' as a purely functional auxiliary.

With other modals and auxiliaries, the main verb version was lost from the language, or became marginal. For example, *will* originally came from a main verb with the sense of volition, but now is almost completely confined to the auxiliary function of marking future tense.

In the Early Modern period, except for *do*, the auxiliary and modal verbs are generally used in the same way as in Present-day English, but sometimes traces of their previous meanings come through more strongly than we are used to. It is rare to find multiple auxiliary verbs in the Early Modern period; constructions like 'The house <u>had been being</u> painted for some time' had yet to develop.

2.1.1 MAIN AUXILIARY VERBS

2.1.1a *Have* and *be*

Historically, *have* and *be* are the main auxiliary verbs in English, showing full auxiliary function from the Old English period on. During the course of the Early Modern period, the verbs are distinguished in their auxiliary roles: *be* is increasingly associated with the formation of passives, and *have* is used to form the present and **past perfect** tenses; for example:

I must <u>be</u> beleed and calmed by him
thou who <u>hast</u> had my purse
thou who <u>hadst</u> had my purse
I <u>have</u> already chosen my officer
I <u>had</u> already chosen my officer

For more on the use of *have* to form the present and past perfect tenses, see section 2.1.4. It is also possible to find *be* in contexts where we would now expect *have*:

[*Troy.*]   What newes *Æneas* from the field to day?
Æne.   That Paris <u>is</u> returned home, and hurt.   (F *TC* 1.1.108–9)

2.1.1b   *Do*

The auxiliary functions of *have* and *be* were established well before the Early Modern period, and have changed only slightly since. *Do*, however, came late to the auxiliary system, and its auxiliary functions develop during the Early Modern period. In Present-day Standard English, auxiliary *do* is used to form questions:

What <u>does</u> she mean by these signs?
<u>Don't</u> you know what this means?

and negative statements and orders:

I <u>do</u> not know why
<u>Do</u> not fear your aunt

It can be added to simple **declarative sentences** to add contrastive emphasis:

I <u>*did*</u> check to see if the lights were off

These functions were present in the Early Modern period, and become progressively more common as the sixteenth and seventeenth centuries go on, but they were in competition with alternative constructions.

   In the case of questions and negatives, *do* formations gradually replace older, *do*-less formations which typically used inversion of the subject and verb:

Simple questions

What <u>does</u> she mean by these signs?
What <u>means she</u> by these signs?

Negative questions

<u>Don't</u> you know what this means?
<u>Know you not</u> what this means?

Negative statements

I <u>do</u> not know why
I <u>know not</u> why
I <u>do</u> not know what you mean
I <u>know not</u> what you mean

Negative orders

<u>Do not</u> fear your aunt
<u>Fear not</u> your aunt

Competition between *do*-formations and *do*-less formations in these contexts begins around 1400 and continues for about three hundred years, with the Present-day system more or less fully in place by 1700.

In the case of simple declarative sentences, a curious anomaly develops: in the second half of the sixteenth century, it becomes possible to add a semantically empty auxiliary *do* to any main verb which does not already have an auxiliary or modal verb in its verb phrase, without any implication of contrastive emphasis:

I went home
I did go home

These unemphatic auxiliary *do* forms reach a peak in frequency around 1600, when on average 10 per cent of simple main verbs have *do* forms added to them. After 1600 the practice declines and disappears.

These changes in the use of *do* mean that users of Early Modern English effectively have two syntactic systems to chose from: one conforming to the Present-day use of auxiliary *do* (termed **regulated**), and one conforming to the older system, including the use of unemphatic *do* in simple declaratives (**unregulated**). Speakers and writers varied in the extent to which they used the regulated system: younger, more educated speakers tended to use a higher proportion of regulated forms, but almost everyone shows some usage of the older forms.

The following extract from *Titus Andronicus* shows the regulated and unregulated systems for *do* use in competition in the work of Shakespeare. I have underlined all verb phrases where *do* either is used, or could have been used. I have marked those instances where unemphatic *do* could have been added to a positive declarative statement with ^. I have also marked two non-auxiliary uses of *do*, and have commented on these at the end of my analysis.

> *Boy.*   Helpe Grandsier helpe, my Aunt *Lavinia,*
> ^Followes me every where <u>I know not</u> why.
> Good Uncle *Marcus* see how swift she ^comes,
> Alas sweet Aunt, <u>I know not</u> what you meane.
>   *Mar.*   Stand by me *Lucius,* <u>doe not feare</u> thy Aunt.   5
>   *Titus.*   She ^<u>loves</u> thee boy too well <u>to doe thee harme</u>.
>   *Boy.*   I when my father was in Rome <u>she did</u>.
>   *Mar.*   <u>What meanes</u> my Neece *Lavinia* by these signes?
>   *Ti.*   <u>Feare not</u> *Lucius,* somewhat <u>doth she meane</u>.
> See *Lucius* see, how much she ^<u>makes</u> of thee: 10
> Some whether would she have thee goe with her.
> Ah boy, *Cornelia* never with more care
> ^<u>Read</u> to her sonnes, then she hath read to thee,
> Sweet Poetry, and Tullies Oratour.
> Canst thou not guesse wherefore she ^<u>plies</u> thee thus?   15
>   *Boy.*   My Lord <u>I know not</u> I, nor can I guesse,
> Unlesse some fit or frenzie <u>do possesse her</u>.   (F *Tit* 4.1.1–17)

The following tables show the regulated and unregulated forms present in the passage for each sentence type:

Positive declarative statements

Regulated	*Unregulated*
my Aunt *Lavinia,* / ^Followes me every where	somewhat <u>doth</u> she meane
how swift she ^comes	Unlesse some fit or frenzie <u>do</u> possesse her
She ^loves thee boy	
how much she ^makes of thee	
Cornelia never with more care / ^Read to her sonnes	
she ^plies thee thus	

Negative statements

Regulated	*Unregulated*
no examples in the passage	I know not why

I know not what you meane

I know not I

Negative orders

Regulated	Unregulated
<u>doe</u> not feare thy Aunt	Feare not *Lucius*

Positive questions

Regulated	Unregulated
no examples in the passage	What meanes my Neece *Lavinia* by these signes?

Other uses of *do*

Titus.   She loves thee boy too well to <u>doe</u> thee harme.
Boy.   I when my father was in Rome she <u>did</u>.

'doe thee harme'	main verb with the lexical content 'perform'
'she did'	substitute (pro-verb) standing for 'loved me'

Although this is not a significant sample, it does illustrate well the way the two systems can be found in one idiolect. Thus we have both regulated and unregulated negative orders, and regulated and unregulated declaratives. Negative statements and questions are represented by only unregulated forms, but could have occurred in regulated structures:

I know not why	→	I do not know why
What means my niece?	→	What does my niece mean?

It is also worth noting that the passage contains a negative question formed using a modal verb:

<u>Canst</u> thou not guesse wherefore she plies thee thus?

This type of construction, established in English long before *do* moved into the auxiliary system, is generally taken to be the model for the shift in functions of *do*. Use of *do* as a dummy auxiliary enabled all questions and negatives to be formed on this structural basis, and maintain *subject–main verb* order, rather than using inversion.

As often in Early Modern English, auxiliary *do* use shows us two systems in competition. What factors affected the choice of regulated or unregulated constructions by speakers and writers? Generally it can be stated that unregulated forms, as the older of the two systems, are more likely to carry formal register. This is certainly the case when Falstaff uses unregulated *do* forms in his pompous Euphuistic parody:

> this pitch (as
> ancient writers doe report) doth defile   (Fp *1H4* 2.4.408–9)

Metrical considerations are also important, since regulated and unregulated versions of the same clause offer writers at least one syllable more or less, and an alternative word order:

> My aunt Lavinia
> Doth follow me everywhere, I do not know why

Here the line 'Doth . . . why' has twelve syllables, with 'everywhere' being placed awkwardly with its second syllable in a stressed position: everýwhere. Contrast this with

> My aunt Lavinia
> Follows me everywhere, I know not why

Here the line 'Doth . . . why' has ten syllables, with 'everywhere' placed so that its first syllable is in a stressed position: éverywhere.

Finally, unregulated auxiliary *do* forms in positive statements often have a discourse-marking function, highlighting the crucial verb in a narrative, or marking a shift in topic (see section 2.1.0 for an example of this in *Othello*).

2.1.2 MODAL VERBS

Type:	can	could
	may	might
	must	
	shall	should
	ought	
	will	would

In Present-day Standard English, modal verbs can only appear as the initial element of a verb phrase which has a main verb as its head. Modals modify the semantic content of the main verb in some way, usually to do with permission, possibility, ability or volition.

Historically, the modal verbs have developed from main verbs, and have undergone significant changes in grammar and semantics. Most differences in the use and behaviour of modals in the Early Modern period can be explained by these changes.

2.1.2a *Can/could*

The original main verb sense of *can* was 'to know something', 'to have knowledge of how to do something', and this sense survives today in Scottish English *ken*. Over time, the meaning of the verb was semantically broadened to include physical ability as well as mental ability. Both senses can be found when the verb is used as a main verb in Shakespeare:

> The summe of all I <u>can</u>, I have disclos'd:
> Why, or for what, the Nobles were committed,
> Is all unknowne to me, my gracious Lord   (F *R3* 2.4.46–8)

That is, 'The sum of all I know'.

> Let the Priest in Surples white
> That defunctive Musicke <u>can</u>,
> Be the death-divining Swan   (Q *PT* 13–15)

That is, 'Who is skilled in funeral music'.

> I have seen my selfe, and serv'd against the French,
> and they <u>can</u> well on horsebacke   (Q2 *Ham* 4.7.82–3)

That is, with a sense of physical riding ability.

2.1.2b *May/might*

Where *can* began with the sense of mental ability, and broadened into physical ability, *may* began with the sense of physical ability (literally 'to have the strength/might to do something'), and shifted into permission and possibility.

In Early Modern English, *might* could still carry its original physical ability sense:

> more he spoke,
> Which sounded like a Cannon in a Vault,
> That <u>mought</u> not be distinguisht   (F *3H6* 5.2.43–5)

> so loving to my Mother,
> That he <u>might</u> not beteene the windes of heaven
> Visit her face too roughly   (F *Ham* 1.2.140–2)

In all of these instances, Present-day English would distinguish the 'physical ability to do something' sense by using *could*. The next example illustrates the semantic ambiguity between 'power to do something' and 'possibility of something being done' which allowed the semantic drift of *might* from actual physical ability to abstract or theoretical possibility:

Isab. Must he needs die?

Ang. Maiden, no remedie.

Isab. Yes: I doe thinke that you <u>might</u> pardon him,

and neither heaven, nor man grieve at the mercy.

Ang. I will not doe't.   5

Isab. But can you if you would?

Ang. Looke what I will not, that I cannot doe.

Isab. But <u>might</u> you doe't & do the world no wrong

If so your heart were touch'd with that remorse,

As mine is to him?   (F *MM* 2.2.48–55)

The possibility sense of *may/might* is strongest now, but *may/might* could also carry the sense of 'permission to do something' in the Early Modern period. Thus, in Present-day English the clause

I may not come

can normally only refer to possibility: 'there is a chance that I will not come'. In Early Modern English, however, the clause is potentially ambiguous with the permission sense also available:

I may not come: 1 'there is a chance I will not come'
                    2 'I am not allowed to come'

In Present-day English, the 'permission' sense would have to be repre- sented by the use of *must* ('I must not come'), but *may* occurs in this sense in Shakespeare:

yet I must not,

for certaine friends that are both his, and mine,

Whose loves I <u>may</u> not drop   (F *Mac* 3.1.119–21)

May and *might* can also be used in Early Modern English to express a wish for something (**optatively**):

Would I <u>might</u>

But ever see that man   (F *Tem* 1.2.168–9)

Lord worshipt <u>might</u> he be   (F *MV* 2.2.89)

2.1.2c *Must*

(See also 2.1.2b.)

Must is derived from the same Old English verb which lies behind *may* and *might*. Like them, its original meaning had to do with physical abil- ity (literally, 'to have the might to do something'), but this spread into obligation. In keeping with the general semantic wanderings of the modals, *must* can be found in Early Modern English in senses which seem to lack direct obligation, and express something closer to simple futurity:

> Hee <u>must</u> fight singly to morrow with *Hector*,
> and is so prophetically proud of an heroical cudgelling,
> that he raves in saying nothing　　　　　　　　(Fp *TC* 3.3.246–8)

2.1.2d　*Shall/should*

Shall can be used as a main verb where there is implied motion (Abbott, 315):

> you Madame <u>shall</u> with us　　　　　　　　　　(F *2H6* 1.4.51)

That is, 'You shall come with us'. Similarly:

> *Cæsar* <u>shall</u> forth　　　　　　　　　　　　　(F *JC* 2.2.10)

That is, 'Caesar shall go forth'.

Should = would

In Present-day English, we can use *would* to refer to habitual action in the past:

> At that time I <u>would</u> go to school every day by bus

Should for us now implies some degree of obligation:

> You <u>should</u> go to school every day

However, just as *will* and *shall* are not clearly distinguished in Early Modern English, so *should* can be used for habitual action:

> Why 'tis well known, that whiles I was Protector,
> Pittie was all the fault that was in me:
> for I <u>should</u> melt at an Offendors teares　　　(F *2H6* 3.1.124–6)

From the context it is clear that what is referred to here are actual events, though in a generalized sense – not what he *ought* to have done when protector, but what he *did* do. Present-day English would require *would* here.

　　Similarly, *should* occurs in Early Modern English in contexts of conditional futurity, with no sense of obligation or desire on the part of the speaker that the events referred to should happen. The most striking instance of this is in *Troilus and Cressida*, in Ulysses' speech warning about the dire effects of undermining order:

> Take but Degree away, un-tune that string,
> And hearke what Discord followes: each thing meetes
> In meere oppugnancie. The bounded Waters,
> <u>Should</u> lift their bosomes higher then the Shores,
> And make a soppe of all this solid Globe:　　　　　　　5
> Strength <u>should</u> be Lord of imbecility,
> And the rude Sonne <u>should</u> strike his Father dead:
> Force <u>should</u> be right, or rather, right and wrong,
> (Betweeene whose endlesse jarre, Justice recides)
> <u>Should</u> loose her names, and so should Justice too　　(F *TC* 1.3.109–18)

Here it is clear that Ulysses does not *want* these things to occur as a result of removing degree (as a modern reading of his *should* forms would imply); he simply asserts that they will happen if degree is lost.

2.1.2e　*Will/would, will/shall*

Auxiliary verb *will* derives from a main verb which meant 'to wish, want', and the sense of volition is still available in Early Modern English:

> I beseech your Majestie give me leave to goe;
> Sorrow <u>would</u> sollace, and mine Age <u>would</u> ease　　(F *2H6* 2.3.20–1)

That is, 'sorrow desires solace', and 'my age desires ease'.

In the following, the first use of *would* carries the main verb sense of volition, while the second functions as an auxiliary verb:

> 　　　　　I <u>would</u> your Highnesse
> <u>Would</u> give it quicke consideration　　(F *H8* 1.2.65–6)

Wanting to do something implies futurity ('I want to go to Spain' implies that I will go at some point in the future), so it is not surprising that 'I will . . . ' structures move from implying the active desire to do something, to denoting simple futurity, even when volition is clearly absent:

> I have no minde of feasting forth to night:
> But I <u>will</u> go　　(F *MV* 2.5.37–8)

At the same time, *shall* (originally with a sense of obligation) was making a similar semantic and grammatical journey into expressing futurity, giving English two analytic futures:

I <u>will</u> go
I <u>shall</u> go

each of which retained the potential to take on its original semantic colouring of volition or obligation. As the auxiliary forms became more and more established, the semantic content of the modals was bleached out, and elision of the auxiliary became normal:

I'<u>ll</u> go

There is a simple register distinction to be made between *shall* and *will* futures: *shall* is formal, and associated with written language; *will* is less formal, and associated with speech. Unfortunately, there is also a much more complex grammatical and semantic distinction to be made: the so-called 'shall/will distinction'.

As a native speaker of Northern British English, the only distinction I intuitively recognize between *shall* and *will* is that *shall* sounds a bit pretentious, and I tend to use it ironically. However, a more complex distinction has been claimed for Southern British English at least since the seventeenth century.

The distinction is based on a tendency (not a rule, and only clearly detectable in more formal written texts) for *shall* to pattern with first person, and *will* to pattern with second and third person. Grammarians in the eighteenth century attempted to fix a semantic distinction onto this grammatical distribution: first person *shall* for simple future, first person *will* for volition; second/third person *shall* for volition on the part of the speaker, second/third person *will* for simple future. Just in case you were in danger of understanding the distinction, these semantic colourations are reversed in questions.

The evidence for any systematic *shall/will* distinction in Early Modern English is not strong. Perhaps there is a distinction in the following:

> *Bru.* Heare me for I <u>will</u> speake.
> Must I give way, and roome to your rash Choller?
> <u>Shall</u> I be frighted when a Madman stares?
> *Cass.* O ye Gods, ye Gods, Must I endure all this?   (F *JC* 4.3.38–41)

Here, the first 'will' has a clear sense of intentionality, and the 'shall' is perhaps simple future. Note too the following:

> *Sicin.* It is a minde that <u>shall</u> remain a poison
> Where it is: not poyson any further.
> *Corio.* <u>Shall</u> remaine?
> Heare you this Triton of the *Minnoues*? Marke you
> His absolute <u>Shall</u>?   (F *Cor* 3.1.85–9)

Though as the Arden 2 editor notes at this point, 'Shakespeare is here attending to a grammatical distinction . . . that elsewhere he usually ignores.'

The variation in the following does not seem explicable:

> And <u>will</u> they so? the Gallants <u>shall</u> be taskt:
> For Ladies; we <u>will</u> every one be maskt.
> And not a man of them <u>shall</u> have the grace
> Despight of sute, to see a Ladies face.
> Hold *Rosaline*, this Favour thou <u>shalt</u> weare,   5
> And then the King <u>will</u> court thee for his Deare:
> Hold, take thou this my sweet, and give me thine,
> So <u>shall</u> *Berowne* take me for *Rosaline*.
> And change you Favours too, so <u>shall</u> your Loves
> Woo contrary, deceiv'd by these removes   (F *LLL* 5.2.126–35)

Nor is it clear to me why the third future form in the following should take *will,* since it seems to be simple future rather than volitional:

> *Ghost.*   To tell thee thou <u>shalt</u> see me at *Philippi*.
> *Brut.*   Well: then I <u>shall</u> see thee againe?
> *Ghost.*   I, at *Philippi*.
> *Brut.*   Why I <u>will</u> see thee at *Philippi* then   (F *JC* 4.3.282–5)

Shall for *if*

It is possible to use *shall* in Early Modern English in contexts where we would require *if* today:

> but <u>shall</u> I speake my conscience,
> Our Kinsman Gloster is as innocent,
> From meaning Treason to our Royall Person,
> As is the sucking Lambe   (F *2H6* 3.1.68–71)

2.1.3 TENSE AND TIME

The relationship between tense and time is not straightforward. Tense is a grammatical feature, while time is a real or imagined state of the world. Consequently, forms grammatically marked for a certain tense do not necessarily refer to the time we associate with that tense. In Present-day English, for example, simple present tense verb forms are more likely to be used to enliven the narration of past events ('I was just sitting there, and he <u>comes</u> up to me and he <u>says</u> . . . ') than they are to be used to refer to events happening in the present. The use of present tense for present events tends to occur only in specialist situations such as sports commentaries:

> Robert with the cross . . . Shearer shoot<u>s</u> . . .and it'<u>s</u> there!

Because of the lack of a one-to-one relationship between tense and time, the following subsections are organized by time, and give examples of the range of tenses and other constructions used to refer to a particular time.

2.1.3a Present time

Early Modern English is far more likely to use simple present tense forms for events taking place at the time of speaking than Present-day English. In the following, Cassius has been sounding Caska out about his plan to depose Caesar:

> But Oh Griefe,
> Where hast thou led me? I (perhaps) <u>speake</u> this
> Before a willing Bond-man: then I know
> My answere must be made. But I am arm'd
> And dangers are to me indifferent.
> *Cask.* You <u>speake</u> to *Caska*, and to such a man,
> That is no flearing Tell-tale   (F *JC* 1.3.111–17)

Both instances of 'speak' here would be more likely to occur as progressive *be* + *-ing* forms in Present-day English:

> I perhaps <u>am speaking</u> this before a willing bondman
> You <u>are speaking</u> to Caska

The progressive *be* + *-ing* construction can be found in Shakespeare, but in contexts which suggest it is informal – prose rather than poetry, comedy rather than tragedy:

> The King he <u>is hunting</u> the Deare,
> I <u>am coursing</u> my selfe.
>   They have pitcht a Toyle, I <u>am toyling</u> in a pytch,
> pitch that <u>defiles;</u> defile, a foule word: Well, set thee
> downe sorrow; for so they <u>say</u> the foole said, and so <u>say</u>
> I, and I the foole: Well proved wit. By the Lord this
> Love <u>is</u> as mad as *Ajax*, it <u>kils</u> sheepe, it <u>kils</u> mee, I a
> sheepe: Well proved againe a my side. I will not love;
> if I do hang me: yfaith I will not. O but her eye: by

5

this light, but for her eye, I would not love her; yes, for   10
her two eyes. Well, I <u>doe</u> nothing in the world but <u>lye</u>,
and <u>lye</u> in my throate. By heaven I <u>doe love</u>, and it hath
taught mee to Rime, and to be mallicholie: and here <u>is</u>
part of my Rime, and heere my mallicholie. Well, she
<u>hath</u> one a'my Sonnets already, the Clowne bore it, the   15
Foole sent it, and the Lady <u>hath</u> it: sweet Clowne, sweeter Foole, sweetest Lady. By the world, I would not care
a pin, if the other three were in. Here <u>comes</u> one with a
paper, God give him grace to grone   (Fp *LLL* 4.3.1–19)

Here, Berowne opens with a string of progressive constructions for
events which are running in the background as he speaks ('is hunting',
'am coursing' 'am toyling'). He switches to simple present tense forms
in the context of universal truths: 'pitch . . . defiles', 'they say . . . ',
'Love is . . . mad'; and retains simple present for an event which sud-
denly occurs: 'Here comes one . . . '. This pattern of usage conforms
closely to Present-day tendencies.

2.1.3b Past time

The range of tenses and constructions used to refer to past time is more
complex than that used to refer to the present, since narrators tend to
have a more complex relationship with the past than with the present.
The following passage from *Othello*, as Iago narrates Cassio's fight with
Rodorigo, shows how narrators can shift in their representations. I have
underlined the verbs in the passage which have past time reference, and
give tense or mood on the right (with a key to the abbreviations below):

This it is Generall:		
Montano and my selfe <u>being</u> in speech,	NFC	
There <u>comes</u> a Fellow, <u>crying</u> out for helpe,	PFP, NFC	
And *Cassio* <u>following</u> him with determin'd Sword	NFC	
<u>To execute</u> upon him. Sir, this Gentleman,	NFI	
<u>Steppes</u> in to *Cassio*, and <u>entreats</u> his pause:	PFP × 2	5
My selfe, the crying Fellow <u>did pursue</u>,	SP + *do*	
Least by his clamour (as it so <u>fell</u> out)	SP	
The Towne <u>might fall</u> in fright. He, (swift of foote)	COND	
<u>Out-ran</u> my purpose: and I <u>return'd</u> then rather	SP × 2	
For that I <u>heard</u> the clinke, and fall of Swords,	SP	10
And *Cassio* high in oath: Which till to night		
I nere <u>might say</u> before. When I <u>came</u> backe	COND, SP	

(For this <u>was</u> briefe) I <u>found</u> them close together	SP × 2
At blow, and thrust, even as againe they <u>were</u>	SP
When you your selfe <u>did part</u> them.	SP + *do* 15

(F *Oth* 2.3.215–30)

Key

NFC	non-finite continuous
NFI	non-finite infinitive
PFP	present for past
SP	simple past
SP + *do*	simple past, with auxiliary do
COND	conditional

Except for Iago's initial 'This it is', every verb phrase here has past-time reference. However, the first past tense verb does not appear until seven lines into the narrative ('did pursue'). Before this, Iago uses non-finite continuous and infinitive forms ('being', 'crying', 'To execute') and present tense ('comes', 'Steppes', 'entreats'). The effect of this non-finite and present-for-past narrative is to collapse any distance between the narrator and the events narrated, stressing the suddenness, and possibly the (supposed) surprise of Iago. Note how the use of continuous forms, and present-for-past, gives the narrative the flavour of 'as it happens' narration: as if events were unfolding before Iago's eyes as he speaks, downplaying his own agency in provoking the fight. The central part of the narrative uses simple past tense with past reference, and the end of this is marked (as the beginning was) with an auxiliary *do* form ('did pursue' and 'did part').

2.1.3c Future time

Strictly speaking, English has no actual future tense, since there is no verb morphology specifically associated with the future in the way that -*ed* marks past tense. Instead, references to future time are most commonly marked by the use of analytic forms such as *will* and *shall* (see section 2.1.2e). Less frequently, future time is represented by present tense forms, often with adverbials making the reference explicit, and sometimes these are mixed with analytic futures:

> *Macb.*   My dearest Love,
> *Duncan* <u>comes</u> here <u>to Night</u>.
>   *Lady.*   and when <u>goes</u> hence?
>   *Macb.*   <u>To morrow</u>, as he purposes.
>   *Lady.*   O never,
> <u>Shall</u> Sunne that Morrow <u>see</u>   (F *Mac* 1.5.58–61)

Who <u>dares</u> receive it other,
As we <u>shall make</u> our Griefes and Clamor rore,
Upon his Death?   (F *Mac* 1.7.78–80)

A number of other constructions can be used with future reference, as the following extract from *Othello* shows (superscript numbers relate to the list below the passage):

Iago. <u>If I can fasten</u>[1] but one Cup upon him
With that which he hath drunke to night alreadie,
<u>He'l be</u>[2] as full of Quarrell, and offence
As my yong Mistris dogge.
Now my sicke Foole *Rodorigo*,   5
Whom Love hath turn'd almost the wrong side out,
To *Desdemona* hath tonight Carrows'd.
Potations, pottle-deepe; and <u>he's to watch</u>[4].
Three else of Cyprus, Noble swelling Spirites,
(That hold their Honours in a wary distance,   10
The very Elements of this Warrelike Isle)
Have I to night fluster'd with flowing Cups,
And <u>they Watch</u>[3] too.
Now 'mongst this Flocke of drunkards
<u>Am I to put</u>[4] our *Cassio* in some Action   15
That <u>may offend</u>[1] the Isle. But here they come.

Enter Cassio, Montano, and Gentlemen.

<u>If Consequence do but approve</u>[5] my dreame,
<u>My Boate sailes</u>[3] freely, both with winde and Streame
                                    (F *Oth* 2.3.44–59)

Of the eight clauses dealing with future events here, there are at least five different constructions:

1   modal auxiliary + infinitive (base form, i.e. without *to*) *can* and *may*

2   auxiliary + infinitive (base form)   *'ll*

3   simple present tense

4   present tense of *to be* + *to* infinitive

5   subjunctive (here in an *if* clause)

Of these constructions, 1, 2 and 3 are still frequent for future in Present-day English, while 4 and particularly 5 are rarer, and restricted to formal registers.

2.1.3d Mixed tense forms

As the examples in section 2.1.3c show, different tense forms with similar time reference can be mixed without apparent incoherence. In some cases, however, Shakespeare exploits the fluidity of the time/tense relationship, mixing tense forms to produce a sense of disorientation. Such a passage occurs as Caesar makes his fateful decision to go to the Capitol (I have noted editorial attempts to rationalize the tense forms below the passage):

> *Cæs.* *Caesar* <u>shall forth</u>; the things that <u>threaten'd</u> me,
> Ne'er <u>look'd</u> but on my backe. When they <u>shall see</u>
> The face of *Cæsar*, they <u>are vanished</u>.
>   *Calp.* . . . a Lionesse <u>hath whelped</u> in the streets,
> And Graves <u>have yawn'd and yeelded</u> up their dead;   5
> Fierce fiery Warriours <u>fight</u>[1] upon the Clouds
> In Rankes and Squadrons, and right forme of Warre,
> Which <u>drizel'd</u> blood upon the Capitoll.
> The noise of Battell <u>hurtled</u> in the Ayre:
> Horses <u>do neigh</u>[2], and dying men <u>did grone</u>,   10
> And Ghosts <u>did shrieke and squeale</u> about the streets
>   (F *JC* 2.2.10–12, 17–24)

1   White (1878): fought

2   F2: did neigh

Here, the tenses do not cohere. Why do we have a simple past in 'the things that threaten'd me' when a simple present is expected in what looks like a statement of universal truth ('the things that threaten me')? Why **present perfect** in 'they are vanished' when future seems to be predicted by 'they shall see'? The conflicting tense forms continue in Calphurnia's speech: 'hath whelped . . . have yawn'd and yeelded' but 'fight'; 'drizel'd' and 'hurtled' but 'do neigh' and then 'did grone'. These confusions produce editorial corrections as early as the Second Folio ('did neigh' for 'do neigh') and in the nineteenth century ('fought' for 'fight'); but a literary case can be made for the stylistic effect of this incoherence, which produces a sense of time being out of joint as Caesar insists on walking into danger.

2.1.4 ASPECT

Along with tense, verb phrases in English can be marked for **aspect**. Aspect has to do with whether or not something has been completed.

Perfect aspect is applied to states or actions completed in the past; **progressive aspect** is applied to states or actions which are seen as unfinished in some way. Thus when Othello is quoted by Iago as saying

I have already chose my officer   (F *Oth* 1.1.17)

the verb phrase carries perfect aspect, because the choice has been made – the action is completed. The past participle, 'chose' (in Present-day Standard English this would be 'chosen' – which is indeed what the Quarto text has here), is what marks the verb phrase as perfect. It would be possible to change the aspect to progressive:

I have already been <u>choosing</u> my officer

where the use of the present participle ('choosing') implies that the action is not yet completed.

Aspect can interact with tense in quite complex ways. For example, it is possible to give continuous aspect to actions begun *and completed* by the time of narration, if their non-completion is relevant to another time within the discourse:

by then I <u>had already been choosing</u> my officer for several days

Aspect is thus a complex feature, related both to the grammatical category of tense, and to the semantic ones of time and relevance. Taking four clauses with perfect aspect (the action is completed in the past in each case), we can see how time and relevance come into play:

simple past	I chose my officer
past perfect	I <u>had</u> chosen my officer
present perfect	I <u>have</u> chosen my officer
future perfect	I <u>will have</u> chosen my officer

Here, each clause encodes a different relationship between the time of choosing (T1), and a second time which is relevant to the time of choosing in some way (T2). The relationship between T1 and T2 can be made explicit by use of a time adverbial (here, 'then', 'by then', and 'by now'):

simple past	I chose my officer (<u>then</u>) T1 and T2 are the same time
past perfect	I had chosen my officer (<u>by then</u>) T2 is a point in the past more recent than T1
present perfect	I have chosen my officer (<u>by now</u>) T2 is the present, T1 is the past

future perfect	I will have chosen my officer (<u>by then</u>)
	T1 and T2 are points in the future, with T2
	further away than T1

This may appear confusing as set out here, but all native speakers of English manipulate this system when they speak (in fact, they manipulate and understand one considerably more complex than the outline given here). A further example from *Othello* may help: in the second line of the play, Rodorigo, in his argument with Iago, complains that Iago has been in a position of trust with him:

Never tell me, I take it much unkindly
That thou *Iago* who <u>hast</u> had my purse,
As if ye strings were thine, should'st know of this   (F *Oth* 1.1.1–3)

Here, 'hast had' is a present perfect – implying that Iago has been able to call on, or look after, Rodorigo's purse in the past, and that he potentially still can at the time of speaking (T2 is the present). If Rodorigo had wanted to signal a decisive break with Iago, he could have said:

Thou Iago who <u>hadst</u> had my purse . . .

where the past perfect, with T2 a point in the past, would have implied that he no longer has access to Rodorigo's purse.

Similarly, when he complains that Othello has passed over him for the lieutenancy, despite his experience of battle, Iago says:

And I (of whom his eies <u>had</u> seene the proofe
At Rhodes, at Ciprus, and on others grounds
Christen'd, and Heathen) must be be-leed, and calm'd
By Debitor and Creditor   (F *Oth* 1.1.28–31)

Iago states that Othello's eyes '<u>had</u> seene' the proof of his ability, using past perfect rather than present perfect '<u>have</u> seen', although the statement is presumably still true at the time Iago speaks. He chooses past perfect, because he is emphasizing that *at the time he made his choice* Othello had seen Iago in battle. The fact that Othello has seen this is not particularly relevant in Iago's present – but it is crucially relevant at the time of the election.

Later in the play, we again get variation between past and present perfect, depending on the relevance of the event represented by the verbal group to the speaker's present:

Cas.   Reputation, Reputation, Reputation: Oh I <u>have</u>
<u>lost</u> my Reputation. I <u>have lost</u> the immortall part of

myselfe and what remaines is bestiall. My Reputation,
Iago, my Reputation.
    Iago. As I am an honest man I <u>had</u> thought you <u>had</u>
<u>received</u> some bodily wound; there is more sense in that
than in Reputation . . . You <u>have lost</u> no Reputation at all
(Fp Oth 2.3.254–62)

Cassio conceives of his loss of reputation as a state which begins in the
past, and continues into the present: he therefore uses the present perfect, 'I <u>have</u> lost'. Iago's dismissal of Cassio's complaint, however, uses
two past perfects: '<u>had</u> thought', '<u>had</u> received', which express a dis-
continuity between the past event and the present. This emphasizes his
change of mind – 'I <u>had</u> thought it was something serious, but now I
see that it isn't.' Iago then switches back to present perfect when
reassessing the relevance of past events to the present: 'You <u>have</u> lost no
Reputation at all'.
    In Present-day English, progressive aspect is marked by use of the
-ing form of the verb (also called the **present participle**):

I am writ<u>ing</u> a book on Shakespeare's grammar

However, constructions like the above are rare in Early Modern
English.
    See also section 2.1.8c on participles.

2.1.4a Simple past for present perfect

Type: I saw him not these many years

In Present-day English, events completed in the past, but with some
relevance in the present, are represented using the present perfect (present tense of *have* and past participle of the main verb):

I <u>have not seen</u> him for many years

Early Modern English allows use of the simple past in such contexts
(especially when the verb is negated):

I <u>saw him not</u> these many yeares, and yet
I know 'tis he   (F *Cym* 4.2.66–7)

I saw not better sport these seven yeeres day   (F *2H6* 2.1.3)

I was not angry since I came to France
Untill this instant   (F *H5* 4.7.57–8)

2.1.5 MOOD

English verbs can carry one of three moods: indicative, subjunctive or imperative. **Indicative** verbs refer to events or processes the speaker conceives of as actual, be they past, present or future. **Subjunctive** verbs refer to events or processes the speaker conceives of as hypothetical or contingent in some way, hence:

> If Consequence <u>do</u> but approve my dreame   (F *Oth* 2.3.58)

where the subjunctive mood is marked by the lack of person agreement on 'do': compare this with the indicative version, 'If consequence <u>does</u> but approve my dream'.

The **imperative** mood is used for orders, and, like the subjunctive, consists of the base form of the verb (in other words, the infinitive without *to*):

> Honest Iago that lookes dead with greeving,
> <u>Speake</u>: who began this?   (F *Oth* 2.3.168–9)

2.1.5a Indicative

> Type: welcome <u>is</u> banishment; welcome were my death

Indicative verbs refer to events or processes the speaker conceives of as actual, be they past, present or future. The following line neatly illustrates the distinction between the actual and the hypothetical:

> Welcome <u>is</u> Banishment; welcome <u>were</u> my Death   (F *2H6* 2.3.14)

Here, the speaker (Eleanor) has just been banished, and this actual state of affairs is represented using the indicative mood, with 'is'. Eleanor then goes on to suggest that she would also welcome death, but since this is a hypothetical, wished-for state, the subjunctive 'were' is used.

Most verbs in any text will be indicative, unless the text is a specialized discourse type (recipes have high frequencies of imperatives). Indicative verbs are the only verbs in Present-day English which carry inflections, though Old and Middle English had specific subjunctive inflections.

Indicative verbs are described more fully throughout this part of the grammar (see, for example, 2.1.0–4, 2.1.8).

2.1.5b Subjunctive

> Type: welcome is banishment; welcome <u>were</u> my death
> (Abbott, 361–71)

The subjunctive mood is used for contexts where the speaker is to some extent uncertain about the reality or likelihood of the events or processes spoken about. Old and Middle English retained specific subjunctive inflections, but by the Early Modern period these had disappeared, and the only formal means for marking the subjunctive was the absence of inflection where it might be expected, or the use of a different inflection from what would be present if the verb was indicative.

The subjunctive has virtually disappeared from Present-day Standard English, only existing in a few lexicalized phrases:

if I <u>were</u> you

Almost all of these lexicalized phrases have indicative counterparts which are now more common:

if I <u>was</u> you

As the above example shows, the subjunctive is now strongly marked for formality, and is associated with writing rather than speech.

Subjunctives are far more frequent in Early Modern English than in Present-day English, and they can be found in the speech of characters from all social ranks, and in all situations. We should not read them as necessarily connoting formality.

The following indicative/subjunctive pairings show the distinctions speakers could make:

Welcome is Banishment; welcome <u>were</u> my Death   (F *2H6* 2.3.14)

Here (as noted in 2.1.5a), the speaker (Eleanor) has just been banished, and this actual state of affairs is represented using the indicative mood, with 'is'. Eleanor then goes on to suggest that she would also welcome death, but since this is a hypothetical, wished-for state, the subjunctive 'were' is used.

A similar contrast is made by the Second Murderer in the same play after the killing of Duke Humphrey:

Oh, that it <u>were</u> to doe: what have we done?   (F *2H6* 3.2.3)

where the murderer specifically wishes that something that has actually been done (the murder), and can be represented with the indicative ('what <u>have</u> we <u>done</u>?'), had not been done yet, and could still be spoken of hypothetically ('Oh, that it <u>were</u> to do').

A wide range of contexts can trigger subjunctive mood, including the following.

Hypotheticals: especially *if* clauses

> *Yorke.*   If *Yorke* <u>have</u> ill demean'd himselfe in France,
> Then let him be denay'd the Regent-ship.
>   *Som.*   If *Somerset* <u>be</u> unworthy of the Place,
> Let *Yorke* be regent, I will yeeld to him.
>   *Warw.*   Whether your Grace <u>be</u> worthy, yea or no,
> Dispute not that, *Yorke* is the worthyer   (F *2H6* 1.3.103–8)

Here, the hypothetical clauses are marked by 'If' twice, and 'Whether'. Note also Warwick's crafty shift into indicative for his assertion that '*Yorke* <u>is</u> the worthyer'.

Prediction of future events: especially *when* clauses

> By flatterie hath he wonne the Commons hearts:
> And when he <u>please</u> to make Commotion,
> 'Tis to be fear'd they all will follow him   (F *2H6* 3.1.28–30)

> Send Succours (Lords) and stop the Rage betime,
> Before the Wound <u>doe</u> grow uncurable   (F *2H6* 3.1.285–6)

Suggestion/optative

The subjunctive can also be used in contexts where the speaker express-es a possible state of affairs which he or she desires:

> *Card.*   . . . What counsaile give you in this weightie cause?
> *Yorke.*   That *Somerset* <u>be</u> sent as Regent thither   (F *2H6* 3.1.288–9)

2.1.5c Imperative

> Type: <u>Speak</u>: who began this?

The *imperative* mood is used for orders, and, like the subjunctive, con-sists of the base form of the verb (in other words, the infinitive without *to*):

> Honest Iago that lookes dead with greeving,
> <u>Speake</u>: who began this?   (F *Oth* 2.3.168–9)

Early Modern English is slightly more likely than Present-day English to have an explicit subject with imperatives (as is found in the previous example), but the most frequent pattern conforms to that of Present-day usage:

<u>Use</u> me but as your spaniell; <u>spurne</u> me, <u>strike</u> me,
<u>Neglect</u> me, <u>lose</u> me   (F *MND* 2.1.205–6)

(See also 2.1.1b on the role of auxiliary *do* in the formation of orders.)

2.1.6 FINITE VERSUS NON-FINITE

Type: *finite*   he <u>loves</u> his own pride
          non-finite   he, <u>loving</u> his own pride

A *finite* verb is one which is marked for tense and person agreement; hence the term finite, since these features are held to limit the scope of the verb. In

But he (as <u>loving</u> his owne pride, and purposes)
<u>Evades</u> them   (F *Oth* 1.1.12–13)

'Evades' is a finite main verb marked as follows:

he   evade<u>s</u>
3rd person singular   *3rd person singular + present tense*

If we change the subject, or the tense, the morphology of the verb changes:

they   evad<u>e</u>
3rd person plural   *3rd person plural + present tense*

they   evad<u>ed</u>
3rd person plural   *3rd person plural + past tense*

In the same sentence, the status of 'loving' is very different, however, since it does not alter form when the person or the tense of the main verb are altered:

I (as <u>loving</u> my own pride and purposes) evaded them
they (as <u>loving</u> their own pride and purposes) will evade them

'loving' is thus a non-finite verb: it is unmarked for tense or person.
    There are three parts of the verb which are non-finite: the *to* infinitive, the *-ing* form and the *-en* form:

I (<u>to love</u> my own pride and purposes) evaded them
I (<u>fearing</u> for my own pride and purposes) evaded them
I (<u>given</u> my own pride and purposes) evaded them

Section 2.1.3b on past time includes an analysis of the effect of non-finite verb forms.

2.1.7 VOICE: ACTIVE/PASSIVE, AGENCY

Type: *active*   I <u>becalmed</u> him

         passive   I <u>was becalmed</u> by him

Verb phrases can be *active,* or *passive.* In an active verb phrase, the entity performing or experiencing the verb (the *agent*) is in the subject position:

subject   *object*

I   know   my price

agent

In a passive verb phrase, however, the agent is in the object position, and the grammatical subject (the noun phrase with which the verb agrees) is the entity which has the verb 'done' to it. Thus Iago's passive sentence

            [I] must be be-leed, and calm'd

By Debitor and Creditor   (F *Oth* 1.1.29–30)

can be represented thus:

subject   *object*

I   must be be-leed, and calmed   by debitor and creditor

                                               agent

since Cassio ('Debitor and Creditor') is the person becalming Iago's career. The statement can be made active by moving the agent into subject position:

subject   *object*

debitor and creditor   belees and calms   me

agent

Passive verb phrases are formed by adding part of *to be* to the *-en* form of the verb:

active   *passive*

I <u>know</u> my price   my price   <u>is known</u> to me

                                        <u>was known</u> to me

                                        <u>will be known</u> to me

2.1.8 VERB MORPHOLOGY

The relatively unstandardized state of Early Modern English is attested by the wide variation found in verb morphology. In fact, the vast majority of verb endings are what we would expect given Present-day standard norms, which were rapidly being established in the Early Modern period; however, a significant number of minority forms survive as a result of historical and dialectal variation. These unusual forms have exercised editors greatly, and the paragraphs dealing with them in Abbott are amongst the most referenced in editions.

2.1.8a Present tense morphology

Second person singular agreement

The expected inflection of the verb with *th*-forms is *-est*, but this can produce clumsy clusters or repetitions of consonants ('thou tormen<u>test</u> me'), and these are often simplified:

Fiend, thou <u>torments</u> me, ere I come to Hell	(F *R2* 4.1.270)
Thou <u>disputes</u> like an Infant: goe whip thy Gigge	(F *LLL* 5.1.60)
Thou now <u>requests</u> but Mooneshine in the water	(F *LLL* 5.2.208)

Third person singular agreement

Type: the great man down, you mark his favourites <u>flies</u>

Instances of apparent third person singular agreement on verbs with plural subjects are common in Early Modern English. In fact, it can be argued that such apparently singular inflections on verbs represent genuine plural agreement: see the following section, 'Third person plural agreement' for an explanation.

Third person plural agreement

Type: the great man down, you mark his favourites <u>flies</u>
(Abbott, 332–40)

One of the constant themes of this grammar is the variation inherent in Early Modern English. Nowhere is this more evident than in verb morphology – in particular in the third person plural present tense slot. As elsewhere in Early Modern English, much of the variation here is due to competition between forms from different dialects of English.

Historically (in the Old and Middle English periods) there were at least four different possible third person plural endings in the present tense:

-es   -en   -th   zero

giving *the men hop<u>es</u>, the men hop<u>en</u>, the men hop<u>eth</u>* and *the men hope*. By the Early Modern period, *zero* (*the men hope*) has established itself as the default form, but *-es*, *-th* and *-en* can still be found in Shakespeare as minor variants.

-es is by far the more frequent of the two minor variants in Shakespeare; for example:

> The great man downe, you marke his favourites <u>flies</u> (F *Ham* 3.2.199)

> The venome clamors of a jealous woman,
> <u>Poisons</u> more deadly then a mad dogges tooth (F *CE* 5.1.69–70)

> My old bones <u>akes</u> (F *Tem* 3.3.2)

These look to us like singular verbs with plural subjects, and they are often inaccurately glossed as such in modern editions. In fact, these are genuinely plural verbs, examples of the feature known as *they* constraint (or, the 'Northern Personal Pronoun Rule').

This rule allows any of the possible plural inflections to appear on verbs which have full noun phrases or relative pronouns as their subjects, but requires *zero* to appear with verbs which have the pronoun *they* as their subject. Note the variation in verb inflections in the following:

> *Troy.* Well know they what they <u>speake</u> that <u>speakes</u>
> so wisely (F *TC* 3.2.150)

Here, the first instance of 'speake' takes *zero*, since its subject is the pronoun 'they', while the second takes *-s*, since its subject is the relative pronoun 'that'.

-th in the third person plural is rarer than *-s* in Shakespeare, but can occur especially if the verb is separated from the subject, with relative pronouns, or if there is verb–subject inversion:

> their Encounters (though not Perso-
> nall) <u>hath</u> been Royally attornyed with enter-change of
> Gifts (Fp *WT* 1.1.26–8)

Here the distance between 'Encounters' and 'hath' may trigger the *-th* inflection.

> I, but I feare you speake upon the racke,
> Where men enforced <u>doth</u> speake any thing (F *MV* 3.2.32–3)

Here the non-finite relative ('enforced') is an encouraging factor (compare: 'Men <u>who have been enforced</u> doth speak any thing').

> <u>Hath</u> all his ventures faild (F *MV* 3.2.266)

Here the verb comes before the subject – something that often triggers third person singular as a default agreement.

-en as a third person plural present tense ending is much rarer than *-s* or *-th* in Shakespeare, and only used in clearly archaic language:

All <u>perishen</u> of man of pelfe   (Q *Per* 2.0.35)

And then the whole quire hold their hips and loffe,
And <u>waxen</u> in their mirth   (F *MND* 2.1.55–6)

As these examples indicate, a range of contexts can increase the likelihood of one of the old plural inflections occurring: verb–subject order; a relative pronoun; a large distance between subject and verb.

Verb–subject order

Verb–subject order seems to make the use of the old plural inflections more likely – though of course there is no absolute way to distinguish these from instances where singular agreement is used as a default since the subject has not been encountered when the verb is produced:

There <u>is</u> no more such Masters   (F *Cym* 4.2.371)

       <u>Is</u> there not Charmes
By which the propertie of Youth, and Maidhood
May be abus'd   (F *Oth* 1.1.171–3)

       <u>Is</u> all things well,
According as I gave directions?   (F *2H6* 3.2.11–12)

       <u>Is</u> there not wars? <u>Is</u>
there not imployment?   (Fp *2H4* 1.2.71–2)

Relative pronouns

See section 1.4.2i.

Coordinated singular nouns as subject

   Type: Faith and troth <u>bids</u> them

Coordinated singular nouns can often take *-s*: presumably whereas Present-day English tends to view such coordinate subjects as two separate things (and hence plural), Early Modern English was prepared to view them as one:

The heavinesse and guilt within my bosome,
Takes off my manhood   (F *Cym* 5.2.1–2)

Where *death and danger dogges the heeles of worth*   (F *AW* 3.4.15)

Thy weale, and wo, are both of them extreames,
Despaire, and hope, makes thee ridiculous   (Q *VA* 987–8)

                         If you can mak't apparant
That you have tasted her in Bed; my hand,
And Ring is yours   (F *Cym* 2.4.56–8)

Apparent cases of plural nouns triggering -s inflections
(Abbott, 337)

Sometimes what looks like a plural noun triggering *-s* on a verb can be explained by the subject's being a noun clause rather than the plural noun:

                the Combatants being kin,
Halfe stints their strife, before their strokes begin   (F *TC* 4.5.92–3)

where 'stints' agrees not with 'Combatants' but with 'the Combatants being kin', so the lines read: 'The fact that the combatants are kin half stints their strife'. Similarly:

Whereon his Braines still beating, puts him thus
From fashion of himselfe   (F *Ham* 3.1.176–7)

                our illes told us
Is as our earing   (F *AC* 1.2.107–8)

And great affections wrastling in thy bosome
Doth make an earth-quake of Nobility   (F *KJ* 5.2.41–2)

2.1.8b Past tense morphology

Type: help–helped
         help–holp

There are two ways of forming the simple past tense in English. The most common one, and the only one that is still productive (that is, the only one available to you if you invent a new verb) is the addition of *-t* or *-ed*. Verbs which follow this pattern are termed *weak*:

walk   walked
type   typed
build   built

However, many core verbs form their past tense by shifting the stem vowel. These are termed *strong* verbs:

run	ran
drive	drove
see	saw
drink	drank

Membership of these two classes has not been stable over the history of English: verbs have jumped between them (especially from strong to weak), and for some verbs, variation still occurs (for example: *hang* → *hanged/hung*; *light* → *lighted/lit*).

Several verbs we now treat as weak had strong past tense forms in Early Modern English:

Three times to day I <u>holpe</u> him to his horse,
Three times bestrid him: Thrice I led him off,
Perswaded him from any further act:
But still where danger was, still there I met him   (F *2H6* 5.3.8–11)

where 'holpe' is the simple past of 'help': 'helped' as it would be in Present-day English. Note also the frequency of other strong verbs in the example: 'bestrid', 'led', 'met'.

2.1.8c Participles

Type:	*-ing* forms	walking	giving	singing	coming
	-en forms	walked	given	sung	come

There are two participles in English: present and past. The present participle ends in *-ing*; past participles end in *-ed* or *-en*, or alter their stem vowel, although some are formed simply using the base form of the verb:

base form	*present participle*	*past participle*
walk	walking	walked
give	giving	given
sing	singing	sung
come	coming	come

Participles have a range of functions. As verbs, they occur with auxiliaries in complex verb phrases:

I was <u>walking</u>
I had <u>walked</u>

I was <u>given</u> a present
He was <u>sung</u> to sleep

Participles are also used as verbs in *non-finite* clauses. This is an important set of subordinate clauses, the two major types of which are **non-finite adverbial clauses** and **non-finite relative clauses**.

Non-finite clauses are significant because they are unmarked for tense (despite the rather confusing terms 'present' and 'past' participle) and because they generally leave the subject of the clause implicit (see the discussion of Iago's use of non-finite clauses in sections 2.0 and 2.1.6).

-*ing* forms (present participles)

-*ing* forms show a cline of behaviour: sometimes they look very like verbs, sometimes they behave more like nouns or adjectives:

Most verb-like

> I see two comforts <u>rysing</u>   (Q *TNK* 2.2.58)
>
> <u>Rising</u> and <u>cawing</u> at the guns report   (F *MND* 3.2.22)

Here the -*ing* forms have fully verb-like behaviour, functioning as the heads of non-finite verb phrases (note in the first example that 'rysing' has an explicit subject: 'two comforts').

Verb-like (but could be replaced by adjectives)

> They are <u>rising</u>   (F *Cor* 4.5.239)

Here, 'rising' is again fully verb-like, appearing as the main verb in a complex present continuous verb phrase which has a subject ('They'). Note, however, the surface similarity of this construction to *to be* + adjective constructions such as:

> They are <u>rebellious</u>

Adjective-like

> with a <u>rising</u> sigh,
> He wisheth you in Heaven   (F *1H4* 3.1.8–9)

Here the -*ing* form shows fully adjectival behaviour, appearing as pre-head modification in a noun phrase ('a rising sigh').

The Prologue of *Henry V* has two *-ing* forms in the same line, the first functioning like a verb, the second like an adjective, but note the active, animating sense of the adjectival use:

Thinke when we talke of Horses, that you see them
<u>Printing</u> their prowd Hoofes i'th'<u>receiving</u> Earth   (F *H5* Prologue 26–7)

Noun-like

the <u>rising</u> of the Mountaine foote   (F *TGV* 5.2.45)

the footsteps of my <u>rising</u>   (F *KJ* 1.1.216)

In both of these instances, the *-ing* form functions as the head of a noun phrase. In the first instance, the *-ing* form is head of the overall construction, and is itself post-head modified by a prepositional phrase:

	Head	*Post-head modification*
NP1(the	<u>rising</u>	PP(of NP2(the Mountaine foote)))

In the second case the *-ing* form is the head noun of a noun phrase which forms part of the post-head modification for another noun:

	Head	*Post-head modification*
NP1(the footsteps		PP(of NP2(my <u>rising</u>)))

-en forms (past participles)

Past participles vary in form far more than present participles because of long-term instability in the English verbal paradigm. In particular, speakers often generalize the base form of the verb, or the simple past tense form, to contexts where we would expect the *-en* form (Abbott, 342, 343):

Farre truer <u>spoke</u> then meant   (F *2H6* 3.1.183)

Queene.   Thrice noble *Suffolke*, 'tis resolutely <u>spoke</u>.
Suff.   Not resolute, except so much were done,
For things are often <u>spoke</u> and seldome meant   (F *2H6* 3.1.266–8)

In all three cases here, the simple past tense form ('spoke') is generalized over the past participle ('spoken'). Similarly:

A man of complements whom right and wrong
Have <u>chose</u> as umpire of their mutinie   (F *LLL* 1.1.167–8)

> He hath not <u>eate</u> paper, as it were:
> He hath not <u>drunke</u> ink   (F *LLL* 4.2.24–5)

In the first example from *Love's Labour's Lost* the simple past tense form, 'chose', is generalized over the *-en* form, 'chosen'. In the second we get an illustration of the wide variation possible in past participle formation: the first past participle is formed using the base form ('eate' rather than 'eaten'), while the second employs the now standard past participle form ('drunke'), rather than the base form ('drink'), or the simple past ('drank').

Note also:

> Hath he not <u>twit</u> our Soveraigne Lady here   (F *2H6* 3.1.178)

where the base form of the verb, 'twit', is used rather than the past participle, 'twitted'.

It is important to remember that many of these instances of what we would regard as non-standard participle formation come from high-status speakers in formal situations: they look 'wrong' to us, but are simply part of the natural variation of Early Modern English (indeed, it may be that forms we now regard as informal and non-standard carried formal or archaic register for Shakespeare).

Past participles tend to appear as nouns only when their adjectival form has been reconverted (for example 'the <u>naked</u> and the dead'). They are frequently found as adjectives however, and this development is logical given their appearance in compound verb phrases with *to be* in contexts where adjectives could also appear:

> I am <u>rob'd</u> sir, and <u>beaten</u>: my money, and ap-
> parrell <u>tane</u> from me   (Fp *WT* 4.3.61–2)

where the participle forms could easily be replaced with full adjectives:

> I am cold sir, and hungry

Archaic past-participle suffix

> Type: <u>y</u>cleped

Early Modern writers (notably Spenser) revived the Old English suffix *ge-* as *y-*, using it to mark participles. Shakespeare only ever uses this as an archaism or in the mouths of characters whose orotund diction he satirizes:

> *Now for the ground Which? which I*
> *meane I walkt upon, it is <u>ycleped</u>, Thy Parke*   (Fp *LLL* 1.1.234–6)

Ped. Judas I am.
Dum. A Judas?
Ped. Not Iscariot sir.
Judas I am, yucleped Machabeus.
    Dum. Judas Machabeus clipt, is plaine Judas   (F *LLL* 5.2.590–4)

2.1.8d Infinitive marking

Early Modern English allows use of the base form, or bare infinitive, in contexts where Present-day English would require use of the infinitive marker *to*:

                 What, know you not
(Being Mechanicall) you ought <u>not ^ walke</u>
Upon a labouring day, without the signe
Of your Profession   (F *JC* 1.1.2–5)

And when your Mistris heares thus much from you,
I pray desire her ^ call her wisedom to her   (F *KL* 4.5.34–5)

As with many features of Early Modern English, the Present-day system is in variation with the alternative:

Worthy *Montanio*, you were <u>wont ^ be</u> civill   (Q *Oth* 2.3.181)

but the Folio has

Worthy Montano, you were <u>wont to be</u> civill   (F *Oth* 2.3.181)

2.1.9 NEGATION

Type: *adverbial*   <u>never</u> tell me
        morphological   <u>un</u>kindly
        grammatical   you'll <u>not</u> hear me
        double negatives   <u>no</u> joy in <u>nought</u>

Negation can be realized by a number of elements, and can appear in a number of different positions in the verb phrase.

The exemplary passage from *Othello* (see 2.0b) shows several of the possible forms of negation:

adverbial – where an adverbial element is added to the verb phrase to negate the verb:

<u>Never</u> tell me   (F *Oth* 1.1.1)

> That <u>never</u> set a Squadron in the Field,
> <u>Nor</u> the division of a Battaile knowes   (F *Oth* 1.1.22–3)

morphological – where a negative affix is added to a word to negate its semantic content:

> I take it much <u>un</u>kindly   (F *Oth* 1.1.1)

> [He] <u>Non</u>-suites my Mediators   (F *Oth* 1.1.16)

grammatical – (1) where a negative particle is added to the verb phrase to negate the verb:

> But you'l <u>not</u> heare me   (F *Oth* 1.1.4)

> If I do <u>not</u>   (F *Oth* 1.1.8)

or (2) by adding a negative determiner to a noun phrase:

> I am worth <u>no</u> worsse a place   (F *Oth* 1.1.11)

> Why, there's <u>no</u> remedie   (F *Oth* 1.1.35)

The examples of type 1 grammatical negation show the two main patterns for ordering elements in a negative verb phrase in Early Modern English:

a.   where an auxiliary is present: *auxiliary verb + negative + main verb* order

But	you	'll	not	hear	me
		auxV	*neg*	*mainV*	

b.   where no auxiliary is present: *main verb + negative* order

If	I	do	not
		mainV	*neg*

The introduction of auxiliary *do* to all negative verb phrases not already containing an auxiliary during the sixteenth and seventeenth centuries pushes this type out of the standard language (see section 2.1.1b).

There is an infrequent third possible negation pattern, in competition with (b), which reverses the positions of the negative and the main verb:

> Yorke, <u>not</u> our old men <u>spares</u>   (F *2H6* 5.2.50)

showing the order

York	not	our old men	spares
	neg		*mainV*

Double negatives

(Abbott, 406)

Double negatives were not generally stigmatized in the Early Modern period, as they were to be in the eighteenth century, and are today. However, they are in decline in the written language before the onset of explicit prescriptivism, and so may be increasingly marked for informality. The repeated negative element adds emphasis:

Live thou to joy thy life;
My selfe <u>no</u> joy in <u>nought</u>, but that thou liv'st   (F *2H6* 3.2.364–5)

Nineteenth-century editorial sensibilities were offended by this line, and 'no' was duly emended to 'to' – an emendation followed by many in the twentieth century.

BEYOND THE HEAD

Verb phrases are structurally far less predictable than noun phrases: a large number of optional elements may or may not appear, and when they do appear they are often highly mobile within the clause. Furthermore, there is a close link between the tensed verb and the subject, an element which is not part of verb phrase structure at all. The optionality and mobility of these elements are frequently exploited in poetic language for formal and semantic reasons: formally, optionality and mobility allow writers to fit words into metrical and other frameworks; semantically, the **fronting** of unexpected elements can shift the emphasis of a line or passage.

The following passage from *The Tempest*, featuring Ferdinand praising Miranda, is structured around three parallel frontings:

> Admir'd *Miranda*,
> Indeede the top of Admiration, worth
> What's deerest in the world: <u>full many a Lady</u>
> I have ey'd with best regard, and <u>many a time</u>
> Th'harmony of their tongues, hath into bondage   5
> Brought my too dilligent eare: <u>for severall vertues</u>
> Have I lik'd severall women, never any
> With so full soule, but some defect in her
> Did quarrell with the noblest grace she ow'd,
> And put it to the foile. But you, O you   10
> So perfect and so peerlesse, are created
> Of everie creatures best   (F *Tem* 3.1.37–48)

The first fronted element here is a noun phrase functioning as an object. A more natural order would be:

subject	*(verb phrase*	*object)*
I	have eyed	NP(full many a lady)

This is echoed by two fronted adverbials:

adverbial	subject		auxV	adverbial	mainV	object
many a time	the harmony of their tongues		hath	into bondage	brought	my ear

adverbial	auxV	subject	mainV	object
for several virtues	have	I	liked	several women

The unusual placement of these elements underlines the parallelism, and the artificiality of the constructions is subtly resolved by the final lines:

> But you, O you
> So perfect and so peerlesse, are created
> Of everie creatures best   (F *Tem* 3.1.46–8)

where 'Of everie creatures best' occupies the most natural clause position, contrasting Miranda's perfections with the awkward failings of other women.

2.2.1 SUBJECTS AND AGENTS

Strictly speaking, the *subject* lies outside the verb phrase altogether:

subject	verb phrase
(Thou)	told'st me thou did'st hold him in thy hate

but there is a close grammatical relationship between the subject and the tensed verb, which must agree with it in terms of person and number. Altering the subject triggers morphological changes on the tensed verb:

subject	verb phrase
He	told me you did hold him in your hate

It is often assumed that the subject is the person or thing which 'does' the verb, but this is not in fact always accurate, since in *passive constructions* (see section 2.1.7), the grammatical subject is the person or thing that has something done to them:

subject	verb phrase
I	must be beleed, and calmed by debitor and creditor

Here, Iago is complaining about being passed in the race for promotion by Cassio (an accountant, hence 'debitor and creditor'), so 'I' is the grammatical subject, but 'debitor and creditor' is the *agent* — the person or thing which steals the wind out of Iago's sails (belees him) and leaves him dead in the water (becalmed).

2.2.2 OBJECTS: DIRECT AND INDIRECT

The role of **direct object** is most usually realized by noun phrases:

I take <u>it</u>	*direct object*
Thou, who hast had <u>my purse</u>	*direct object*
If ever I did dream of <u>such a matter</u>	*direct object*

Some verbs allow or require two objects, which behave slightly differently from each other, and are termed *direct* and **indirect objects**:

	direct object	*indirect object*
Thou told'st	<u>(me)</u>	<u>(thou did'st hold him in thy hate)</u>

Here, 'tell' functions as a **ditransitive verb** with two objects (you generally tell someone something): the first object is 'me', a pronoun noun phrase; the second object is 'thou did'st hold him in thy hate', a noun clause. We can check this by substituting 'it' for the whole of this clause:

Thou told'st (<u>me</u>) (it)

Direct and indirect objects behave differently in a number of ways. Generally, when their positions are reversed, the indirect object will take a preposition such as *to*:

Thou told'st (it) (<u>to</u> me)

and indirect objects are usually easier to delete than direct objects (though this instance is not a very good example of this):

Thou told'st (it)
?Thou told'st (<u>me</u>)

The following gives a better sense of this tendency:

I gave (<u>you</u>) (<u>my purse</u>)
I gave (<u>my purse</u>) (<u>to you</u>)
I gave (<u>my purse</u>)
*I gave (<u>you</u>)

2.2.3 COMPLEMENTS

The role of **complement** can be realized either by an adjectival phrase or by a noun phrase:

As if the strings were <u>thine</u>   *possessive adjective*
<u>Mere prattle without practice</u> is all his soldiership *noun phrase*

Complements differ from objects in their relationship to the subject of the clause. Where objects tend to be different entities from the subject of their clause, complements tend to be identical with, or attributes of, the subject. A fairly restricted set of verbs take complements: *to be, to seem, to become* are the main ones. As the second example shows, it is usually fairly easy to **front** complements by switching them with the subject (and vice versa):

As if <u>thine</u> were the strings
<u>All his soldiership</u> is mere prattle without practice

Such moves are frequently made for metrical reasons as well as emphasis in Shakespeare.

2.2.4 ADVERBIALS

Type: think, <u>when we talk of horses</u>, that you see them
          some kinds of baseness are <u>nobly</u> undergone
          I'll carry it <u>to the pile</u>

Adverbial elements can consist of *adverbial clauses*:

Thinke <u>when we talke of Horses</u>, that you see them
Printing their prowd Hoofes i'th'receiving Earth   (F *H5* Prologue 26–7)

adverbial phrases:

          Some kindes of basenesse
Are <u>nobly</u> undergon   (F *Tem* 2.2.2–3)

and *prepositional phrases*:

Ile carry it <u>to the pile</u>   (F *Tem* 2.2.25)

Adverbials, as the above examples show, modify the verb phrase in some way, and there are two key elements to their behaviour. Most significantly, they are highly mobile, and can usually be moved to several different locations within their clause:

think, <u>when we talk of horses</u>, that you see them
<u>when we talk of horses</u> think that you see them
think that you see them <u>when we talk of horses</u>

some kinds of baseness are <u>nobly</u> undergone
some kinds of baseness are undergone <u>nobly</u>
<u>nobly</u> are some kinds of baseness undergone

I'll carry it <u>to the pile</u>
<u>to the pile</u> I'll carry it
I'll <u>to the pile</u> carry it

This mobility has an obvious advantage for the writing of metrical verse, in the alternative word orders it allows, but there is a semantic resource here too, since the placing of an adverbial in an unexpected position will tend to stress the modifying element:

<u>to the pile</u> I'll carry it

Here, the adverbial has been fronted, with the implication that the destination is significant in some way.

The second feature of the behaviour of adverbials is that they are usually deletable without making the resulting clause ungrammatical:

think that you see them
some kinds of baseness are undergone
I'll carry it

GLOSSARY

These definitions are provided as an aid to readers, and are not meant to be comprehensive. Readers who want to investigate these terms more fully should consult David Crystal's *A Dictionary of Linguistics and Phonetics* (Blackwell, 2003, 5th edition) and Katie Wales's *A Dictionary of Stylistics* (Longman, 1990, 2nd edition).

accusative
A grammatical case associated with nouns functioning as objects, marked with inflections in Old and Middle English, but surviving in Early Modern and Present-day English only on some pronouns (*I* → *me*).

active
A clause or verb phrase in which the subject is also the agent: *I saw the battle*. Compare this with the passive version: *The battle was seen by me*, where the agent (*me*) is the object.

Active can also be applied to adjectives. An adjective used in an active sense is best paraphrased with an active clause: *the extensive view* → *the view extends over a large area*. Active adjectives can be contrasted with passive adjectives, which are best paraphrased with a passive clause: *the extendable bookcase* → *the bookcase can be extended*.

adjectival phrase
A unit of analysis, since adjectives can themselves be pre-modified by intensifiers: *The red lips* → *The very red lips*. The functional equivalence of *red* and *very red* is recognized by classifying both as adjectival phrases.

adjective
A word used to describe an attribute of a noun. Adjectives can occur within the noun phrase as pre-head (attributive) or post-head (postpositive) modification: *The red lips* versus *The lips red*. Adjectives also occur outside the noun phrase as complements (predicative position): *The lips were red*.

adverb, adverbial
A somewhat loosely defined category, the central members of which typically specify the action of a verb: *He did it quickly*. Adverbs generally relate to aspects such as the way something is done, the place it is done, and the time it is done. Adverbial elements are typically highly mobile and/or deletable: *He did it quickly* → *He quickly did it* → *Quickly he did it* → *He did it*.

adverbial clause
The same function as adverbs and adverbial phrases, but adverbial clauses include a subordinate verb: *He did it while thinking about something else*.

adverbial phrase
A unit of analysis, since adverbs can themselves be pre-modified by intensifiers: *He did it quickly* → *He did it very quickly*. The functional equivalence of *quickly* and *very quickly* is recognized by classifying both as adverbial phrases.

agent, agency
The agent is the entity in a clause which actually performs the action defined in the verb. In an active clause, the agent and subject are the same: *I saw the battle*. In a passive clause, however, the agent is the object: *The battle was seen by me*.

alveolar fricative
A sound made by partially constricting the air flow through the mouth: the tip of the tongue is placed close to the alveolar ridge, just behind the teeth. Found at the start of words such as *snake* (voiceless) and *zebra* (voiced).

analytic
A means of conveying grammatical information using word order and function words rather than inflections. Over time, English has shifted to being more and more analytic, hence subject and object roles are marked by word order, not inflection.

antecedent
The previously occurring element to which a pronoun refers. In the following example, *that* and *it* are pronouns which both refer back to their antecedent, *the book*: *I read the book that she gave him. It was rubbish.*

apposition
Two units in clause structure which share a grammatical role and have the same reference, most frequently found with pairs of co-referential noun phrases: *Nigel Fabb, the professor of linguistics, will lecture today at 2.00.*

article
A type of determiner used in English to distinguish specific or definitely known nouns (*the* book) from unspecific or indefinitely known nouns (*a* book).

aspect
A category marked on English verbs which interacts with tense. Aspect has to do with relative states of completion of the action of the verb. Progressive aspect implies incompletion or continuing relevance: *I have been writing about it for some time.* Perfect aspect implies completion at some point in the past: *I had written about it in 1996.*

attributive
A type of placement of adjectival phrases, where the adjectival phrase comes immediately before the noun it modifies: *The red lips.*

auxiliary verb
A subset of verbs which can occur in the verb phrase alongside a main lexical verb. The main auxiliary verbs in English are *be, do* and *have* (*I am finished, Did you finish, Have you finished*). The modal auxiliary verbs include *can/could, will/would, may/might* (*I can read, I will send you it, You might find this useful*).

base form
The infinitive of the verb without *to*. Used for the simple present tense (except third person singular) and imperatives, amongst other contexts.

clause
A syntactic unit, normally containing at least a subject and a verb phrase: *I ran. She saw the battle.* Imperative clauses may contain only a verb phrase: *Listen!*

closed class
The term for a class of words which very rarely gets new members. Closed classes tend to be grammatical, or functional, for example prepositions. Contrasts with open classes, such as nouns.

comparative

Adjectives in English can be made comparative either by the addition of an inflection (synthetic) or by using the adverbs *more, less* (analytic): *I chose the thicker book. I chose the book which was more weighty.*

complement

An element of clause structure occurring with a restricted set of verbs in English (such as *to be, to seem, to become*). Complements resemble objects, but tend to be attributes of the subject, rather than different entities (as is the case with objects). Hence complements are often adjectival phrases, though noun phrases occur in this role too: *The battle was fierce. He became king. She seemed amused.*

conversion

The use of a part of speech in a different role. Very common in English, and possible in almost any combination: noun → verb (*Fax me the details*); adjective → verb (*He reddened at this*); preposition → adjective (*The down escalator*); pronoun → adjective (*The he-man*).

count noun

A type of noun which can be pluralized, and which can be counted using whole numbers (*one horse, two horses, three horses*). Can be contrasted with non-count nouns, which usually cannot be pluralized, and refer to substances assessed, for example, by weight (*a pound of butter, two pounds of butter*).

dative

A grammatical case originally used in Old and Middle English for a variety of functions, most to do with complex or subsidiary (e.g. indirect) objects. All dative inflections were lost in English during the Middle English period, and distinctive dative and accusative pronouns fell together. Thus dative survives with reference to constructions where the dative case would have been used, but no longer is owing to loss of inflections and/or distinction, e.g. 'ethical' dative: *Knock me this door here.*

declarative sentence

A sentence which asserts a proposition (as opposed to a negative declarative, or a question, or an imperative): *She saw the battle.*

definite article

A type of determiner used in English to distinguish specific or definitely known nouns (*the* book) from unspecific or indefinitely known nouns (*a* book).

deictic, deixis
A linguistic process whereby items refer either to the context of production of a piece of text (*now, here, this, I, you*) or to other elements previously mentioned (*The dog that I told you about*).

demonstrative
A function word which can function either as a determiner (*This one is the best*) or as the head of a noun phrase (*I'll take that, please*). Demonstratives also have a deictic function.

dental fricative
A sound made by partially constricting the air flow through the mouth: the tip of the tongue is placed between the teeth. Found at the start of words such as *thigh* (voiceless) and *the* (voiced).

determiner
A closed class of function words including articles (*a/an, the*), demonstratives (*this, that*), and quantifiers (*some, many*). Determiners function in noun phrases to specify the reference of the noun in some way.

direct object
The main, undeletable object of a transitive verb: *I gave him the present*. Distinguished from the indirect object, which can be deleted, or may be marked with a preposition: *I gave the present. I gave the present to him*.

discourse marking
The use of a feature which signals a transition from one section of discourse to another in some way. Typical discourse markers are expressions such as *Well . . . , In conclusion . . . , So . . . , Now . . .* Other features can be used as discourse markers.

displaced
Adjectives can have different scopes, or location of effect. Localized adjectives refer to a quality inherent in the noun they modify: *The green door*. Displaced adjectives refer to a quality inherent in an implied second party: *A fearful danger* (i.e. 'A danger which makes someone afraid').

ditransitive verb
A verb which takes a direct and an indirect object: *I gave him the present*.

double marking
The process of marking information twice: for example, plurality is marked by the quantifier and the inflection on *two horses*.

Early Modern English
The form of English used between *c.* 1450 and *c.* 1700. Characterized by almost complete absence of Old and Middle English inflections, and rapid standardization of written form up to and immediately after 1600. Many features show competition between two or more means of expression (e.g. *thou/you* in second person singular pronoun).

elision
The reduction of a word or words by dropping a sound or sounds: *over* → *o'er, I will* → *I'll*.

ellipsis
The omission of a word or words from a clause or phrase: *I saw him and* ^ *went over to him*.

-*en* form
A form of the verb whose main function is as the past participle. So named as many past participles end in -*en*: *The sermon was given. He had been driven to drink. The words were written on the wall*. However, note that many do not: *I was saved. She got divorced*.

ethical dative
Strictly speaking neither ethical nor dative, a construction found in Early Modern English where a pronoun appears after the verb, looking very like some kind of object: *I am appointed him to murder you*. Usually expressed in Present-day English in a *by* or *to* prepositional construction: *I am appointed by him to murder you*.

finite relative clause
A relative clause containing a finite verb phrase: *My friend Denis, who lives in Leeds, is a keen boxer*. Can be contrasted with non-finite relatives, which contain a non-finite verb: *My friend Denis, living in Leeds, is a keen boxer*.

finite verb
A verb which has tense and number agreement (and hence is limited, or made finite in reference): *I went there. He goes there*. Distinguished from non-finite verbs, which show no tense or number agreement: *While going there I thought about you. While going there he thinks about you*.

form

Literally the shape or appearance of a word, usefully distinguished from function, since words can shift function without changing form. Thus, *driven* is an *-en* form, but can function as a past participle or an adjective: *The horse was <u>driven</u>. The <u>driven</u> horse.*

front, fronting

The movement of an element from its expected place in a clause to the front. Especially common in verse, and especially likely to happen with complements (<u>*Happy*</u> *we are*) and adverbials (<u>*That Whitsun,*</u> *Jennifer was late getting away*).

function

What a word or phrase does, rather than what it looks like. Usefully distinguished from form, since words can shift function without changing form. Thus *driven* is an *-en* form, but can function as a past participle or an adjective: *The horse was <u>driven</u>, The <u>driven</u> horse.*

function word

Also termed a grammatical word: a word with a purely grammatical function, lacking reference to something in the real world. Contrasts with lexical word, which has semantic content and real-world reference. Thus articles (*a/an, the*) and prepositions (*to, under, on, at*) are function words, while nouns are lexical words.

functionally equivalent

Used of two different entities which have the same grammatical function. Thus in the following two clauses, the bare noun *Richard* is functionally equivalent to the noun phrase *My brother, who lives in Edinburgh*: <u>*Richard*</u> *got married to Katie. <u>My brother, who lives in Edinburgh,</u> got married to Katie.*

future perfect

A verb phrase combining the future tense (*will*) with perfect aspect (*-en* form of the verb), implying that the action or state referred to in the verb will have been completed by a certain time: *I <u>will have chosen</u> my officer.*

future tense

English has no morphological future (in the sense that the form of the verb changes to indicate future tense, as it does for past), but instead uses an analytic construction, combining the base form of the verb with an auxiliary (usually *will*): *I will go and see Kellie and Mike in London.*

genitive
A grammatical case used to express possession. The *-s* marker added to English nouns is one of the few remaining inflectional endings in English: *Shakespeare's Grammar*. A non-case marked analytic alternative also exists in English, employing a preposition: *The Grammar of Shakespeare.*

given information
A phrase used when describing the information structure of sentences, referring to information which is assumed to be known by the recipient of a text, or which has recently been communicated. Elements which constitute given information are often represented by function words (e.g. pronouns): *I sent the book to Laura. She will tell me what is wrong with it.*

grammatical word
Also termed a function word: a word with a purely grammatical function, lacking reference to something in the real world. Contrasts with lexical word, which has semantic content and real-world reference. Thus articles (*a/an, the*) and prepositions (*to, under, on, at*) are function words, while nouns are lexical words.

head
The most important word in a phrase, usually impossible to delete. Gives its name to the phrase, and the phrase is functionally equivalent to the head. Verb phrase head: *I saw the battle*. Noun phrase head: *I saw the battle*. Prepositional phrase head: *I saw the battle in my mind's eye.*

head-shifted relative clause
A type of relative where some element of clause structure comes between the head of the noun phrase that the relative modifies and the relative clause. Rare in Present-day written English, but still found in speech, and common in Early Modern English: *The man hates me who lives over there.*

high-register item
A vocabulary item carrying formal, technical or archaic connotations. Usually derived from Latin or French, and often paired or tripled with

neutral or low-register items derived from Old English or Germanic sources. For example: *king* (neutral), *monarch* (high register).

idiolect

The version of a language characteristic of one individual, a somewhat restricted subset of the total available resources of a language at any one point. For example, Shakespeare's idiolect shows less use of Latinate neologisms than the idiolects of most other writers in the Early Modern period.

imperative

Mood of the verb used to convey orders. Formed using the base form of the verb: <u>Go</u> *home!* <u>Listen</u> *to me!*

indefinite article

A type of determiner used in English to distinguish unspecific or indefinitely known nouns (<u>a</u> *book*) from specific or definitely known nouns (<u>the</u> *book*).

indicative

Mood of the verb used in making statements: *I <u>saw</u> the battle.* Can be contrasted with other moods, such as imperative (<u>See</u> *the battle!*).

indirect object

The secondary, deletable object of a transitive verb: *I gave <u>him</u> the present* → *I gave ^ the present.* Distinguished from the direct object, which cannot be deleted (**I gave him* ^). May be marked with a preposition: *I gave the present <u>to him</u>.*

infinitive

Non-finite form of the verb; may appear as the base form, with no marking (*listen, feel, be*), or marked with the preposition *to* (*to listen, to feel, to be*).

inflection

An inflection is a morpheme carrying a piece of grammatical information which is added to the end of a word. Thus *-s* is a plural inflection (*horse* → *hors<u>es</u>*) and *-ed* is a past-tense inflection (*walk* → *walk<u>ed</u>*).

-ing form

Non-finite form of the verb with a wide range of possible functions; appears as present participle (*I was <u>going</u> home*), and can easily be converted into a noun (*The <u>going</u> was rough*).

levelling
Process found in the shift of English from an inflectional (synthetic) language to an analytic one: where previously several different endings were used to mark the same case or grammatical feature, with time they are 'levelled' to leave only one remaining. For example, various Old English plural inflections are levelled in the Middle English period until only -s remains, and is used in almost all contexts.

lexical word, lexical noun, lexical verb
Contrasts with function or grammatical word: a word with semantic content and usually some kind of real-world reference. For example: *book, horse, jump, fight*. Grammatical words lack semantic content: *the, an, this, that*.

lexicalization
The process whereby a feature being lost from the language generally is retained in one formulaic context, so that what had originally been a part of the grammatical system is fixed (lexicalized) on only one word or only a very few words. For example, the Old English zero morpheme plural is lexicalized on words such as *sheep* and *deer*, but lost from the grammatical system as a whole.

localized
A term used to specify the scope of an adjective. Localized adjectives refer to a quality inherent in the modified noun: *The green door.*

location of effect
Adjectives can have different scopes, or location of effect. Localized adjectives refer to a quality inherent in the noun they modify: *The green door.* Displaced adjectives refer to a quality inherent in an implied second party: *A fearful danger* (i.e. 'A danger which makes someone afraid').

main verb
The head of the verb phrase in the main clause of a sentence, as opposed to any verbs in subordinate clauses: *While polishing my armour, I heard the sound of battle.*

marked
A term used of the minority linguistic variant in any case where users have a choice of linguistic features to perform the same function. Usually implies that its selection has to be motivated in some way, and if motivation is not present the unmarked, or default, term will be used.

For example, in Early Modern English there are two possible forms of the second person singular pronoun. The marked form is *thou*, which is less frequent than the unmarked, *you* form. *Thou* is almost always motivated in some way, whereas *you* can often be entirely neutral.

Middle English
The form of English used between *c.* 1100 and *c.* 1450. Characterized by rapid loss of Old English inflectional morphology, and rise of alternative, analytic constructions. Written versions are characterized by a high degree of dialectal diversity.

modal verb
A type of auxiliary verb used to communicate various different modifications to the meaning of the main verb. Can express futurity (*will*), ability (*can*), permission and obligation (*may, should, ought*).

modification
The process of specifying or altering the reference of a word in some way. Nouns are typically modified by adjectives: *The green door*. Verbs can be modified by adverbs (*He did it quickly*) or modal verbs (*He might do it*). Adjectives can be modified by adverbial intensifiers: *The very green door*.

mood
A set of contrasting parts of the verb used to express different types of meaning. Indicative mood is the default mood, used for statements and questions: *I saw the battle. Did I see the battle?* Imperative mood is used for orders: *See the battle!* Subjunctive mood is very rare in Present-day English, but was more extensively used in Early Modern English to express a range of meanings associated with hypotheticals and possibility: *If I were to see the battle . . .*

morpheme
The smallest collection of letters (or sounds) which still has meaning. Can be a bound morpheme, which only exists attached to other morphemes (*walk-ed, im-proper, small-est*), or a free morpheme, which can exist independently (*walk, bird, go, small*).

morphemic level gloss
A representation of a phrase or clause where each morpheme is glossed to make the grammatical structure of the words clear.

morphology

The resources a language has to show grammatical relationship by changes in a word's form (e.g. by inflections). Old English had a very rich morphology, with numerous different inflections communicating various types of grammatical information. Present-day English has a much reduced morphology, but examples are plural -s (*book* → *book̠s*), third person singular present tense -s (*I listen* → *she listen̠s*), past tense -ed (*You walk* → *you walk̠ed*).

nasal

The sound made by making a complete closure of the airway in the mouth, and expelling air through the nose. Found at the start of *nasal* (closure made at alveolar ridge) and *mother* (closure at lips), and at end of *sing* (closure made at velum).

negation

The process by which a sentence can be brought to express the opposite of what was originally said. Can be achieved by adding a negative quantifier to a noun phrase: *I bought no̠ biscuits*. Can also be achieved by adding a negative particle to the verb phrase: *I did not̠ buy biscuits*.

negative particle

Added to the verb phrase to make it negative: *I bought biscuits* → *I did not̠ buy biscuits*.

new information

A phrase used when describing the information structure of sentences, referring to information which is new to the recipient of a text. Elements which constitute new information are usually represented by full noun phrases: *I sent the book̠ to Laura̠. She will tell me what is wrong with it.*

nominative

A grammatical case associated with nouns functioning as subjects, marked with inflections in Old and Middle English, but surviving in Early Modern and Present-day English only on some pronouns (*I̠* → *me*).

non-count noun

A type of noun which usually cannot be pluralized, and which refers to substances assessed, for example, by weight (*a pound of butter̠, two pounds of butter̠*). Can be contrasted with count nouns, which can be pluralized: *One horse̠, two horses̠, three horses̠.*

non-finite adverbial clause
An adverbial clause containing a non-finite verb: *Musing on the frailty of life, I walked over the battlefield.*

non-finite relative clause
A relative clause containing a non-finite verb phrase: *My friend Denis, living in Leeds, is a keen boxer.* Can be contrasted with finite relatives, which contain a finite verb: *My friend Denis, who lives in Leeds, is a keen boxer.*

non-finite verb
A verb which does not have tense or number agreement (and hence is not limited, or made finite in reference): *While going there I thought about you. While going there he thinks about you.* Distinguished from finite verbs which do show tense and number agreement: *I went there. He goes there.*

non-restrictive relative clause
A relative clause which contains information not essential to identifying the noun modified by the relative. Restrictive relative clauses contain information essential to identifying the noun correctly. I have only one brother, so when I say, 'My brother, who lives in Edinburgh, got married to Katie', the relative clause 'who lives in Edinburgh' is non-essential information, and is thus non-restrictive. If I had two brothers, one in Edinburgh and one in Helsinki, the relative would become essential to identifying which brother had married Katie: 'My brother who lives in Edinburgh got married to Katie'.

non-subject
A term used by linguists to refer to what would previously have been called accusative. The usage is based on the theory that case has virtually disappeared from English, with nominative still being recognized, but all other roles classed by speakers as 'non-subject'.

noun
A type of word used to refer to things (*table, computer, radio*), people and places (*Ruth, Jonathan, Carbondale, North Shields*), and a wide range of abstract entities and states (*love, happiness, anger, sweetness*).

noun clause
A clause which is functionally equivalent to a noun phrase: *Shutting the door was my first mistake → It was my first mistake.*

noun phrase
A term used in analysis which recognizes the functional equivalence of bare nouns, and nouns accompanied by determiners and modification: *Shergar was missing* → *The famous racehorse which had won so many races was missing.*

object
Traditionally defined as the entity in a clause which has the verb done to it. Usually placed after the verb in an active clause, and before it in a passive clause: *I saw the battle* → *The battle was seen by me.*

Old English
The form of English used between *c.* 500 and *c.* 1100. Characterized by a rich inflectional morphology, and relatively unfixed word order. A series of written standards were established and replaced during the Old English period as the power of different kingdoms grew and declined.

optative
Expressing a wish or desire: can trigger the subjunctive in Early Modern English.

palatal fricative
The sound made by making a partial closure of the mouth with the tongue at the soft palate. Found at the start of *shame* (unvoiced) and in the middle of *measure* (voiced).

passive
A clause where the object is fronted, formed by adding part of *to be* to the verb phrase: *I saw the battle* → *The battle was seen by me.*
    Passive can also be applied to adjectives. An adjective used in a passive sense is best paraphrased with a passive clause: *the extendable bookcase* → *the bookcase can be extended.* Passive adjectives can be contrasted with active adjectives, which are best paraphrased with an active clause: *the extensive view* → *the view extends over a large area.*

passivized
Used of adjectives modifying nouns in circumstances where the meaning can best be paraphrased using a passive clause. Thus *My desert unmeritable* can be paraphrased *My desert, which is unable to be rewarded.*

past-for-past narration
A narrative of events which occurred in past time using the past tense: *I saw the goal, I shot, and I scored!*

past perfect
Combination of the past tense and perfect aspect: *I had chosen my officer.* Carries the sense that the state or action of the verb had been completed by some explicit point in the past.

past tense
A tense of the verb closely associated with events which occurred in past time (though there is not a one-to-one relationship between tense and time). Most English verbs form their past tense by adding -ed (weak verbs), though a significant minority shift their central vowel (strong verbs): *I walk → I walked. I sing → I sang.*

perfect aspect
A feature marked on verbs relating to the state of completion (or otherwise) of the event or state referred to by the verb. Perfect aspect implies completion, and contrasts with progressive aspect, which implies incompletion: *I had chosen my officer → I had been choosing my officer.*

phrase
A group of words which function together in clause structure, having the function associated with the head word.

post-head modification
Noun-phrase modification which is placed after the head noun. Normally relative clauses or prepositional phrases (*The car that I wanted was too expensive. The car in the window was too expensive*), but occasionally adjectival (*The car, silver, was calling me from the showroom window*).

postpositive
The placement of modifying adjectives after the head noun of a noun phrase: *Strike out this jelly vile.*

predicative
The placement of modifying adjectives outside the noun phrase after the verb (usually the verb *to be*): *The jelly was vile.*

pre-head modification
Noun phrase modification which is placed before the head noun. Normally adjectival: *The vile jelly.*

preposition
A grammatical word, often referring to place, possession and direction: *to, at, with, of, under.*

prepositional phrase
A phrase governed by a preposition, with a noun phrase embedded in it: *to the lighthouse.* Generally prepositional phrases function either as post-head modification (*The car in the window*), or as adverbial elements (*In the window, the car looked great*).

Present-day English
Form of English used in the present (i.e. late twentieth century and early twenty-first century). Characterized by a high degree of analysis, and slow rates of grammatical change. The standard written version is very precisely fixed, and shows little variation compared with past states of the language.

present-for-past narration
A narrative of events which occurred in past time using the present tense: *I see the goal, I shoot, and I score!*

present participle
Non-finite *-ing* form of the verb, used to convey progressive aspect, amongst other things: *I had been choosing my officer.*

present perfect
Combination of the present tense and perfect aspect: *I have chosen my officer.* Used to imply that a process begun in the past has been completed before the time of speaking.

present tense
The tense of the verb associated with present time, though Present-day English uses the present tense readily for past events (*So I goes up to him and I says . . .*) and future events (*I fly to Seattle in April*).

progressive aspect
A feature marked on verbs relating to the state of completion (or otherwise) of the event or state referred to by the verb. Progressive

aspect implies incompletion, and contrasts with perfect aspect, which implies completion: *I had been choosing my officer* → *I had chosen my officer.*

prolepsis
A rare and specialized usage of adjectives whereby an attribute the modified noun will have if something happens is represented as if it were already an attribute of the noun: *I will slice off your head, and with your blood stain the discoloured ground.*

pronoun
A grammatical word used in place of a full noun phrase. Pronouns depend on shared knowledge, since the recipient of a text must be able to recover their reference. Hence they are common in speech, where context is shared, and generally mark given information in written texts: *My friend Denis lives in Leeds. He is a keen boxer.*

pronoun replacement
The process of replacing full noun phrases with pronouns.

quantifier
A type of determiner which specifies the head noun in terms of how much of it is present: *some, any, no, many.*

recessive
Used in relation to competing forms in a situation of language change to refer to the form which is in decline. Thus using inversion to form questions (*Saw you the battle?*) is recessive during the Early Modern period, with auxiliary *do* constructions eventually replacing this method entirely (*Did you see the battle?*).

referent
The noun or noun phrase to which a pronoun refers: *Jessica is meeting us tonight, isn't she?*

regulated
Used of sentence formation to refer to the now standard use of auxiliary *do* in statements, negatives and questions (i.e. auxiliary *do* only used for contrastive emphasis in statements, but obligatory in questions and negatives if no other auxiliary is present): *No you're wrong — I did see her. Did you see her? I did not see her.*

relative clause
A subordinate clause which acts as post-head modification in a noun phrase: *The books that I took on holiday disappointed me.*

relative pronoun
A pronoun found at the start of finite relative clauses referring to the noun that the clause modifies (the antecedent). The main relative pronouns in English are: *who(m), which, that, zero.* Other words which can function as relative pronouns include: *where (The place where we meet must be secret), when (The day when that happens will be your last), what* (non-standard English: *The man what I know is called Billy), as* (non-standard English: *The woman as knows him is Clara).*

restrictive relative clause
A relative clause which contains information essential to identifying the noun modified by the relative (the antecedent). Can be contrasted with non-restrictive relatives, where the information contained in the relative clause is not essential to identifying the antecedent. For example, I have only one brother, so when I say, '*My brother, who lives in Edinburgh, got married to Katie'*, the relative clause '*who lives in Edinburgh'* is non-essential information, and is thus non-restrictive. If I had two brothers, one in Edinburgh and one in Helsinki, then the relative would become essential to identifying which brother had married Katie: '*My brother who lives in Edinburgh got married to Katie'.*

scope
Used of adjectives functioning as noun modifiers to define the location of the attribute referred to by the adjective. Most adjectives refer to an attribute inherent in the modified noun (localized scope): *The green book.* But some adjectives can be used to refer to attributes which the noun evokes in other entities (displaced scope): *A fearful task.*

semantic
In its widest sense, to do with the meaning content of all words, but more frequently used in this grammar in a restricted sense contrasting with grammatical or functional. Words with semantic content are taken to have some kind of real-world reference (for example nouns, adjectives and verbs: *bread, green, chortle*) while grammatical or functional words have reference within texts and function to make grammatical relationships clear (for example determiners: *the, an, this, that*).

sentence fragment
In written texts, something punctuated as a sentence, but lacking a main verb: _Midnight_. _Flickering lights_. _Dogs to the left of me_. I gulped air and began to run.

sentential relative clause
A relative clause which has a whole clause as its antecedent, rather than just a noun phrase: _I said I would pay for everything, which turned out to be a mistake_.

split genitive
A genitive construction where the head noun (the thing possessed) is placed between an initial _s_-genitive and a final _of_ genitive. The final _of_-genitive modifies the noun of the initial _s_-genitive: _The ladies hearts of France_. In Present-day English, the two genitive constructions are brought together to form a group genitive: _The ladies of France's hearts_.

strong verb
A verb which forms its past tense by altering its central vowel, rather than adding -_ed_: _sing_ → _sang_, _write_ → _wrote_, _speak_ → _spoke_.

subject
Traditionally defined as the entity in a clause which does or experiences the verb. Usually placed before the verb in an active clause, and after it in a passive clause: _I saw the battle_ → _The battle was seen by me_.

subjectivization
A general process of language change whereby words shift from conveying objective facts about things to expressing the subjective opinion of the speaker. In this grammar, used in relation to adjectives which often in Early Modern usage retain their pre-subjectivized, objective sense. Hence _probable_ can be used in Early Modern English to mean 'giving objective proof', 'proving', where its Present-day sense has to be the subjectivized 'seems to me to be likely'.

subjunctive
Mood of the verb used in Early Modern English in a range of contexts, generally to do with states and events which are hypothetical in some way, or about which the speaker is unsure. Often used in contrast with the indicative: _Oh that it were to do: what have we done?_ (Here, a murderer regrets his actions, using the indicative for something that has

happened – *what have we done?* – and subjunctive to express the wish that the action was still hypothetical or potential: *Oh that it were to do.*)

synthetic
A means of conveying grammatical information using inflections rather than word order and function words. Over time, English has shifted from being a highly synthetic language to being more and more analytic.

tense
A feature marked on verbs, associated with the time at which the events or states referred to took place; thus there are present, past, and future tenses. The relationship between time and tense is complex, however (English readily uses present tense forms to refer to past and future events).

to infinitive
A non-finite form of the verb, made up of the base form of the verb and the preposition *to*: *to eat, to sleep*.

transitive verb
A type of verb which is ungrammatical unless accompanied by an object: **He gave ^* versus *He gave a book*.

unmarked
A term used of the majority linguistic variant in any case where users have a choice of linguistic features to perform the same function. Usually implies that its selection does not have to be positively motivated. For example, in Early Modern English there are two possible forms of the second person singular pronoun. The marked form is *thou*, which is less frequent than the unmarked, *you* form. *Thou* is almost always motivated in some way, whereas *you* can often be entirely neutral.

unregulated
Used of sentence formation to refer to the now lost means of forming questions and negatives without auxiliary *do* (*Saw you the battle? I saw not the battle*) and to include non-emphatic use of auxiliary *do* in statements (*Then I did go home*).

velar stop
A sound made by making, then releasing, a complete closure of the airway, using the back of the tongue at the velum. Found at the start of *king* (voiceless) and *grunge* (voiced).

verb

A word referring to a state or action, which can carry features such as tense, aspect, mood, and so on: *be, seem, fax, build.*

verb phrase

For the purposes of this grammar, taken to include everything in a clause apart from the subject. Headed by the main verb, and auxiliary if present, and potentially also including direct and indirect objects, complement, adverbials.

voice

A feature of clauses, divided into active and passive. Active voice has the subject in the initial position in the clause; passive voice brings the object to the front of the clause. Active: *I saw the battle.* Passive: *The battle was seen by me.*

weak verb

A verb which forms its past tense by the addition of *-ed: walk → walked, hope → hoped, floor → floored.*

zero-morpheme derivation

The process of shifting the class of a word without adding an explicit derivational affix. For example, adjectives can be made into nouns using the suffix *-ness: red → red<u>ness</u>* (*I saw the redness stain the water*). But it is also possible to use the bare form of the original word in a new function, in which case linguists postulate the addition of an 'invisible' zero morpheme: *I saw the <u>red</u> stain the water.*

LIST OF REFERENCES TO SHAKESPEARE'S WORKS

INDEX